OBSTACLE COURSE

THE REPORT *of the* TWENTIETH
CENTURY FUND TASK FORCE *on the*
PRESIDENTIAL APPOINTMENT PROCESS

OBSTACLE COURSE

With background papers by
G. Calvin Mackenzie
and Robert Shogan

1996 ◆ The Twentieth Century Fund Press ◆ New York

ᴮᴶᴼ 8314-0/1

ᴴe Twentieth Century Fund sponsors and surpervises timely analy-
s of economic policy, foreign affairs, and domestic political issues.
ᴼt-for-profit and nonpartisan, the Fund was founded in 1919 and
ᴵdowed by Edward A. Filene.

Library of Congress Cataloging-in-Publication Data

Obstacle course : the report of the Twentieth Century Fund Task Force on
the presidential appointment process: with background papers / by G.
Calvin Mackenzie and Robert Shogan.
  p.   cm.
  Includes bibliographical references (p.   ) and index.
  ISBN 0-87078-401-3
  1. United States–Officials and employees–Selection and appointment.
2. Presidents–United States.   3. United States. Congress. Senate.   I.
Mackenzie, G. Calvin. II. Shogan, Robert. III. Twentieth Century Fund.
Task Force on Presidential Appointments.
JK731.U54 1996
353.001'325–dc20   96-27236
                      CIP

Cover design, graphics, and illustration: Claude Goodwin
Manufactured in the United States of America.

FOREWORD

On paper, few groups of Americans look as good as presidential appointees. Regardless of party, those selected for high federal posts are likely to be exponentially above average in terms of educational and professional attainment. Most have been tested in difficult jobs in the private sector, academia, or at other levels of the government. Moreover, it is common for appointees to take substantial pay cuts in order to perform public service. Yet, rather than being praised for their past accomplishments or willingness to join the public sector, many appointees encounter opposition that forces them to run a gauntlet of critical political, press, and legislative scrutiny. For some unlucky high profile nominees, an apparent transformation takes place, as all previous success is set aside and the focus of attacks upon their selection narrows to a few newsworthy or at least controversial rumors or facts about their lives. Overall, a significant fraction of appointees finds the disclosure, clearance, and confirmation process a difficult, sometimes even destructive, experience.

Today, prospective appointees have to fill out a half dozen disclosure forms detailing all aspects of their personal and financial history—from the birthplaces of parents-in-law to the itemization of every source of income going back more than a decade. Waivers have to be signed allowing the FBI and the IRS to root around at will. This effort to find anything that might be used by opponents to embarrass the president seems clearly out of hand—except when one considers the negative reactions to unforeseen questions related to housecleaning and child care.

In recent years, a handful of pending appointees have been challenged on grounds that seem to give credence to the worst parodies of the public sector. They have been vilified by their opponents as a distasteful amalgam of cretins, ideologues, sex maniacs, draft dodgers, tax evaders, illegal alien employers, or alcohol abusers. For whatever reasons, the liturgy on correct comportment and the checklist of relevant questions for public officials has evolved in sensational ways. Combined with increased press attention, the new standards of fitness for public office seem to have soured the citizenry rather than reassured it. The altered ground rules for appointees also may be deterrents to participation in public life by our most qualified and experienced citizens. Anyone watching what happened to Senator John Tower, Clarence Thomas, Zoë Baird, and Kimba Wood might be forgiven for giving public service a wide berth. This is not to say that alcoholism, sexual harassment, conflict of interest, or tax cheating are not legitimate topics to consider in assessing fitness for office.

Perhaps it is no coincidence, therefore, that, by the beginning of the 1990s, the average time it took for a presidential appointee to be confirmed had lengthened to eight and a half months (compared to two months during the Kennedy administration). Conversely, the average period such an appointee served in office had shortened to just over two years. Regardless of one's partisan persuasion, it is obvious that this is no way to run a national government.

With these developments in mind, the Twentieth Century Fund decided to gather a group of distinguished and knowledgeable Americans to consider possible reforms in the process of selection, clearance, and Senate confirmation of presidential appointees. We were conscious of the intensity of the political stakes, the organizational inertia, and the media scrutiny that shapes the appointment process today. We were aware, as well, that many perceptive observers think that nothing can be done to change the emerging pattern of increasing conflict about the very basic task of staffing an administration. But we also were convinced that a considerable number of influential people in both the major parties and the press are troubled by the heightened conflict about so many positions. Moreover, we heard ample anecdotal evidence to the effect that the current process was intrusive and even unfair for many potential and actual nominees. The substantial contribution made to our thinking by G. Calvin Mackenzie of Colby College, who wrote one of the background papers and served as executive director of this Task Force, added to our conviction that the right group might be creative and effective on this issue.

The Task Force set itself a high hurdle, seeking to advance under-standing and provide some guidance for those who serve in the pub-lic sector, either as elected officials or as government employees, as well as those in the media who report on and, in a sense, judge gov-ernmental activities. As the Report that follows demonstrates, the Task Force that was eventually assembled fulfilled our high hopes.

The Task Force, which included several members with direct per-sonal experience in the appointment and confirmation process, ben-efited from additional perspectives provided by Robert Shogan of the *Los Angeles Times*, who wrote the other background paper, and, along with former *Washington Post* reporter Paul Taylor and Ken Auletta of the *New Yorker*, discussed media-related issues with the members of the Task Force. Tom Korologos, long-time Washington political advis-er, also helped the Task Force by explaining to the members how nominees prepare for the confirmation process.

Ultimately, the members reached a consensus on a surprising number of issues, perhaps suggesting that there is more room for bipartisan progress in this area than recent history would suggest. In addition to practical suggestions focused on how a new administration might improve the appointment process during and immediately after a presidential transition, the Task Force recommended a num-ber of steps, the implementation of which would require agreement between the White House and the Senate. Included in this category are suggestions for changes in the clearance procedures and forms, streamlining of some aspects of the Senate confirmation process, and even a few changes in relevant statues. Taken as a whole, the Task Force's conclusions represent, in essence, a bipartisan call for more common sense and goodwill—a plea for a renewed willingness to get on with the job of providing good government.

On behalf of the Trustees of the Twentieth Century Fund, I thank the Task Force members, and especially the co-chairs, former Senators John Culver and Charles McC. Mathias, for their strong contributions to this ongoing and important debate.

RICHARD C. LEONE, PRESIDENT
The Twentieth Century Fund
September 1996

CONTENTS

MEMBERS OF THE TASK FORCE

John C. Culver, *Task Force Co-Chair*
Partner, Arent Fox Kintner Plotkin & Kahn; former U.S. Senator

Charles McC. Mathias, *Task Force Co-Chair*
President and Chairman, First American Bankshares, Inc.;
former U.S. Senator

John Brademas
President Emeritus, New York University; former U.S. Congressman

Suzanne Braun Levine
Editor, *Columbia Journalism Review*

Arthur B. Culvahouse, Jr.
Managing Partner, O'Melveny & Myers, LLP; former Counsel to
President Ronald Reagan

Lloyd N. Cutler
Senior Counsel, Wilmer, Cutler & Pickering; former Counsel to
Presidents Jimmy Carter and Bill Clinton

Amy Gutmann
Dean of the Faculty, Princeton University

Charles V. Hamilton
Wallace S. Sayre Professor of Government, Columbia University

Constance Horner
Guest Scholar in Governmental Studies, The Brookings Institution;
former Head of the U.S. Office of Personnel Management for President
Ronald Reagan; former Director of the Presidential Personnel Office
for President George Bush

Thomas H. Kean
President, Drew University; former Governor of New Jersey

Arnie Miller
Principal, Isaacson Miller; former Director of the Presidential
Personnel Office for President Jimmy Carter

John D. Podesta
Visiting Professor of Law, Georgetown University Law Center; former
White House Staff Secretary for President Bill Clinton

Theodore C. Sorensen
Senior Partner, Paul, Weiss, Rifkind, Wharton & Garrison; former
Special Counsel to President John Kennedy

Michael I. Sovern
President Emeritus and Chancellor Kent Professor of Law, Columbia
University

Richard J. Tofel
Director of International Development and Administration, Dow
Jones & Co., Inc.

Paul A. Volcker
Former Chairman of the Board of Governors, Federal Reserve Board

John C. Whitehead
Former Deputy Secretary of State

G. Calvin Mackenzie, *Task Force Executive Director*
Distinguished Presidential Professor of American Government, Colby
College

REPORT OF THE TASK FORCE

The American public's trust in the federal government began to decline during the Vietnam War, plummeted after Watergate, and subsequently continued to deteriorate. Over that same period, not coincidentally, the scrutiny of presidential nominees for executive branch service steadily intensified as the insistence on greater accountability escalated. The clearance process for those asked to serve at the upper levels of government has grown to unimagined levels of complexity and redundancy, often complicated by fierce political partisanship. Senate consideration of nominees becomes at times a chamber of horrors where respectable Americans suddenly find their integrity called into question, their credentials disparaged, and their reputations permanently threatened. Individuals who agree to serve in a presidential administration face an appointment process that is increasingly dominated by "win-at-any-cost" politics, media feeding frenzies, and a sharp decline in public civility.

Of course, it is essential to take prudent steps to ensure that government officials are capable, honorable, and worthy of public trust. The constitutional provision requiring Senate advice and consent for presidential appointments and the long-standing practice of extensive background checks are intended to ensure that insufficient scrutiny does not contribute to government malfeasance and incompetence. The question is whether those basic safeguards have mutated into a system that no longer serves the purposes for which it is intended.

The Twentieth Century Fund convened a bipartisan Task Force on the Presidential Appointment Process to assess whether the current system, on balance, is beneficial or detrimental to good government. The central conclusion of the Task Force is that the confirmation process is undermining the very trust in government it is supposed to foster. It often disables the government as key appointments languish and federal agencies and departments go without leadership for months—even years—at a time. In addition, many talented and honorable candidates for office decide against serving because of the intrusiveness of the process.

At a time when the need for public services is great, when the demand for efficiency and effectiveness is justifiably strong, when the problems government confronts are growing in complexity—that is, at a time when creative leadership is as important as it has ever been—the principal American mechanism for providing that leadership is in disarray. The presidential appointments process generally served America well for most of our history, but it no longer does—at least not as it currently operates.

The Task Force believes that the procedures used to fill the highest offices in the federal service must by altered significantly. Failure to do so now will result in further deterioration of the appointment process and deeply aggravate a decline in the leadership of federal agencies and departments.

The stakes are high. Nearly two million civilian employees work in the executive branch of government. But only two of them are elected by the American people: the president and the vice president. Most of the rest are career civil servants who look to several thousand political appointees for policy guidance and leadership. Those appointees play a critical role in defining and implementing public policy, in managing and inspiring the federal workforce, and in keeping government responsive to the people it serves. When the quality of those political appointees declines, or they are not available because of delays in selection, nomination, and confirmation, every facet of federal operations suffers.

The Task Force has focused on several particularly important flaws in the contemporary appointment process. These are explored more fully in the background papers that follow this Report, but a summary here sets the context for the Task Force's recommendations.

▲ *The appointment process is too slow.* The two most recent presidential transitions—one with a Republican succeeding another Republican, the other with a Democrat succeeding a Republican—took much too long to unfold. President Bush and President Clinton were many months into their presidencies before their leadership teams were fully

in place. On average, appointees in both administrations were confirmed more than eight months after the inauguration—one- sixth of
an entire presidential term.

Compare this to the presidential transition of 1960. Kennedy
appointees were confirmed, on average, fewer than two and a half
months after the inauguration. But each president after Kennedy has
had to wait longer than his predecessors to get his administrative
team in place. The process is now so routinely slow, whether at the
outset or during the term, that long vacancies in senior administrative
positions have become a normal condition of Washington life. In
every agency and department at any given moment, some leadership
positions are vacant, while others are filled by holdovers from previous
administrations or temporary place-holders. Important decisions are
postponed; caseload backlogs accumulate. When Mary Schapiro was
finally confirmed to head the Commodity Futures Trading Commission in October of 1994, for example, she became the agency's
first permanent chief in twenty-one months.

And while presidents wait, so do the people they appoint.
Sometimes they wait for months on end in a limbo of uncertainty and
awkward transition from the private to the public sector. Some simply give up. Tired of waiting for the appointment process to conclude,
Anne Hall withdrew as a nominee for a Republican seat on the board
of the Federal Deposit Insurance Corporation in 1994. When Stanley
Tate withdrew after waiting four months for the Senate to confirm his
appointment to head the Resolution Trust Corporation, he called
those months the "most difficult and stressful involvement" of his life.

In political time, windows of opportunity quickly close. When
presidents are unable to fully exercise leadership simply because they
have no administrative team to back them up, the quality of government performance is diminished and the public trust erodes further.
Yet this is now the norm. The new president takes office promptly
on January 20, but the president's team trickles in slowly over the following year. The momentum of the election dissipates before there
are leaders in place to translate it into policy initiatives.

▲ *The appointment process is repellent to the very people it seeks to recruit.*
Many of America's most creative leaders and technical specialists
decline opportunities for public service because they do not want to
submit to the appointment process. They see it as an obstacle course

that assumes guilt rather than innocence, that invites inappropriate public scrutiny, that encourages a relentless politics of brutality, that invades privacy and demolishes reputations. Even Americans who would relish the opportunity to contribute their talents to their country, and who would do so at great financial sacrifice, are unwilling to endure an appointment process that they have come to regard as a meat grinder.

The United States has long benefited from the public service of distinguished citizen-leaders—people who have worked in the private sector as well as in government. But today there are powerful disincentives in the appointment process that make such people hesitate to accept a call to public service. Presidential advisers responsible for recruiting appointees now report increasing difficulty in attracting their top choices for many positions. Nearly all recent studies of the appointment process report the same finding. It took President Bush twelve months to fill the position of commissioner of the Food and Drug Administration, eighteen months to get a director of the National Institutes of Health, and twenty-two months to put in place a director of the Office of Energy Research. The evidence is powerful and consistent: putting America's top talent at work in the public service is harder today than it has been at any previous time, and it grows steadily more difficult—in significant part because of flaws in the appointment process.

▲ *The appointment process is often abusive to appointees.* Even those Americans willing to accept an invitation to join a presidential administration soon learn the high and often unanticipated costs of public service. They are required to answer dozens of probing questions about their personal lives: Have they ever used drugs? Have they ever been in psychological counseling? Have they ever had an abortion? Have they ever rented a pornographic film? What is their credit history? What potential skeletons hang in their closets? They have to undergo a thorough reckoning and revelation of their personal and family finances. Their views on important policy issues are subject to intense scrutiny. Teams of FBI agents scour the country talking to former associates and neighbors, searching for any information that might be used to question the candidate's qualifications or embarrass the candidate and the president if made public.

Then comes Senate confirmation. A new investigatory process unfolds, often repeating much of what has already occurred. More weeks and months pass. Some nominees become objects of rumor or criticism during this time. Others may become pawns in political debates that have nothing directly to do with them or the office they've been selected to fill. For months in 1995, for example, the Senate Foreign Relations Committee refused to act on fifteen ambassadorial nominations as its chairman sought an agreement with the president on a restructuring plan for the State Department. Some nominations become flash points in already pitched political battles over issues like civil rights (William Lucas, William Bradford Reynolds, Lani Guinier) or abortion (C. Everett Koop, Henry Foster). At these moments, the gloves come off and nominees are often subject to innuendo, exaggeration and misrepresentation of views, and character assaults.

Of course, intense scrutiny and extensive public disclosure are appropriate in the process of evaluating the men and women who will wield vast power in the offices for which they have been nominated. But the problem is that, far too often, the examination process wanders far afield from that necessary evaluation. As a result, nominees are robbed of their legitimate right to privacy and the nation is robbed of their service.

▲ *The appointment process has become a maelstrom of complexity, much of which serves little public purpose.* The Appendixes to the Report (see page 169) include a selection of the forms and questionnaires that all political appointees must now execute. Those materials give overwhelming testimony to the excesses of the appointment process. There are too many questions, too many forms, too many clearances and investigations and hearings. The appointment process is too slow because it is too cumbersome and redundant. It is repellent to potential appointees and abusive to those nominated because it is so often unnecessarily intrusive and humiliating. Simplicity, clarity, and a focused sense of the public interest have vanished from the appointment process. Presidents, appointees, and the American people all suffer as a result. President Clinton himself has argued that "it's time to have a bipartisan look at this whole appointments process. It takes too long to get somebody confirmed. It's too bureaucratic. You have two and three levels of investigation. I think it's excessive."

The Task Force believes it is possible to correct many of the flaws that beset the current appointment process and produce so much frustration in presidents and such profound anxiety in nominees.

The members of the Task Force envision an appointment process that is simple and sensible, that informs the public of nominees' qualifications and character, that concentrates the bulk of its attention on the most significant appointments, that matches the level of scrutiny to the level of risk, and that treats Americans willing to serve their country with respect and civility. The following recommendations are offered as practical steps to secure an appointment process that balances appropriate scrutiny and caution with the public interest in an efficient and effective process of leadership selection and retention.

RECOMMENDATIONS

The recommendations that follow focus on four principal areas: the scope of the appointment process, the recruitment and nomination process, the Senate confirmation process, and the need for greater civility.

SCOPE OF THE APPOINTMENT PROCESS

The number of presidential appointments should be substantially reduced, by approximately a third of the current total.

The American approach to staffing top executive-branch positions seeks to encourage a constant flow of new energy and ideas into government and to ensure the responsiveness of the senior officers of the government to the president and to the president's electoral mandate. Over the years, however, the number of presidential appointments, especially those requiring Senate confirmation, has been growing. Part of the growth is attributable to an increase in the number of government agencies and departments, part to the steady addition of new layers of upper-middle management, and part to the conversion to presidential appointments of positions previously in the civil service or appointed by others.

The painful consequence is that the appointment process is now overwhelmed by the burden of all these complex personnel choices. Many months pass before new administrations are in place. In-term vacancies often last for a half-year or more. Candidates for appointment are kept on hold for months while their appointments are "processed." Leadership teams are in constant flux. It's no way to run a railroad, let alone a large modern government.

Many of the Task Force's recommendations are aimed at making the appointment process more efficient, rational, and timely. But we must first confront the major cause of contemporary difficulties. The process is swamped. If presidential appointments are ever to possess the prestige and visibility necessary to attract and retain the country's very best talent, there must be fewer of them. So must there be fewer if we are to accomplish the more careful selection and aggressive recruitment that modern administrations require. The current large number of presidential appointments undermines both objectives.

The reduction recommended here would have the additional benefit of strengthening America's beleaguered civil service. The National Commission on the Public Service reported in 1989 that "Too many of our most talented public servants . . . are ready to leave. Too few of our brightest young people . . . are willing to join." Reducing the number of presidential appointments will improve the appointment process while simultaneously increasing opportunity, raising morale, and enhancing the appeal of careers in public service. This reduction would be good for the president, good for appointees, good for the public service, and good for the country.

Appointments to most advisory commissions and routine promotions of military officers, foreign service officers, public health services officers, except those at the very highest ranks, should cease to be presidential appointments and cease to require Senate confirmation.

The Constitution states that the president "shall nominate, and by and with the advice and consent of the Senate, shall appoint ambassadors, other public ministers and consuls, judges of the Supreme Court, and all other officers of the United States, whose appointments are not herein otherwise provided for, and which shall be established by law; but the Congress may by law vest the appointment of such inferior officers, as they think proper, in the president alone, in the courts of law, or in the heads of departments."

In the early days of the republic the government was tiny and a president could easily pay attention to the appointments and promotion of nearly all its employees, including military officers at every rank. The practice of treating these as presidential appointments requiring Senate confirmation took early root.

It is a practice the nation outgrew long ago. While such routine appointments and promotions consume little of the time and attention of busy modern presidents and senators, they clutter the appointment process with reams of unnecessary paper. The Task Force believes, as a sound general principle, that the president should bear direct responsibility for the appointment of only those officials who have a reasonable likelihood of interacting with him or of working directly on presidential business. Genuine presidential appointments should not be confused with other categories of personnel appointment and promotion. The Task Force similarly believes that the Senate should not be burdened with confirmation responsibilities for appointments or promotions that almost never rise to the level of senators' attention. Following that principle, the Task Force believes that both branches should be relieved of the antiquated practice of treating routine military, foreign service, and public health service promotions and appointments as presidential appointments requiring Senate confirmation.

The Task Force notes the importance, however, of certain exceptions, again following the principle stated above. Senior military appointments to positions with major command or important staff responsibilities and chief of mission appointments in the foreign service should continue to be presidential appointments requiring Senate confirmation.

RECRUITMENT AND NOMINATION PROCESS

The Presidential Personnel Office, Counsel to the President's Staff, Office of Government Ethics, and other relevant investigatory agencies should be augmented with additional, temporary staff to help process the extraordinary appointments burden when a new president takes office.

Presidential transitions are a time of overload in the appointments process. Hundreds of important posts must be filled quickly. In recent transitions, this process has stretched to intolerable lengths. One way to accelerate and improve the transitions between administrations is to add temporary staff to manage them more efficiently. This change would allow the affected agencies to conduct their routine tasks for many appointments simultaneously and meet the special burdens that occur during a transition. The staff augmentations should last no more than the six months following an inauguration.

This temporary staff should include individuals with special responsibility for media relations. Rumors, false reports, and other forms of misinformation swirl around the appointment process in a presidential transition. The Task Force believes that new administrations have an obligation to keep the media as fully informed as possible about appointment news. A special media relations office or officer should be assigned the task of providing information and responding to daily press questions during the transition. This media office would be the central source and contact point for information on presidential appointments and would work closely with media relations officers in the individual departments and agencies. A central, well-informed media contact point would serve the public's right to know about these important decisions and would also help to protect candidates for appointment from false rumors and misinformed allegations.

FBI full-field investigations should be eliminated for some appointments and substantially revised for others.
The FBI full-field investigation became a routine of the appointment process in the early 1950s. It quickly spread to all appointments and took on a life of its own. But full-field investigations are rarely a high priority for the FBI and rarely produce that agency's best work. Successive presidents have bemoaned the length of time these investigations require. White House staffs have often criticized the jumble of highly intrusive and frequently uncorroborated information they produce. FBI files sometimes leak, to the embarrassment of nominees or their patrons, and full-field investigations require a large and inefficient allocation of FBI resources that could be applied to better purposes.

There is no justification for maintaining the FBI full-field investigation for all appointments. The Task Force believes that all nominees must be persons of integrity and that appropriate checks must be undertaken to ensure that. The Task Force also believes that the backgrounds and character of appointees in highly sensitive positions involving national security must be checked more thoroughly than any others. But the FBI full-field investigation is simply too blunt and intrusive an instrument for the purposes for which it is currently used. It should be retained for sensitive posts, but for most other positions it should be replaced with a more efficient, less intrusive, and more useful background check conducted by the FBI or by a small, new agency created for the primary purpose of performing this routine investigative function. The Task Force suggests the nature of that agency in a recommendation that follows. For part-time, per diem, and other minor positions where there are no genuine national security considerations, the Task Force believes that the FBI full-field investigation can be eliminated altogether.

The current conflict of interest laws should be amended to simplify the task of identifying potential financial conflicts of interest.

The Task Force favors extensive public financial disclosure by nominees for presidential appointment. But disclosure should be a simple process for nominees, and it should yield clear and useful information about potential conflicts of interest.

The current ethics laws require candidates for appointment and all senior appointees to file financial disclosure reports (SF 278) that mandate the reporting of income and assets in numerous categories of value. This requirement imposes large burdens on the filers because income and asset values are inherently moving targets. An asset's value today may place it in a different category from its value yesterday. Nominees and appointees often report the difficulty they encounter and the time they—and often their accountants and attorneys—expend trying to file such reports accurately.

The Task Force finds no significant purpose in retaining the current reporting categories. The public interest would be satisfied and appointee inconvenience greatly relieved by simplifying the reporting requirements. The Task Force believes this goal can best be accomplished by the establishment of a single conflict-of-interest threshold or de minimis level. All assets would be reported; their value need only be indicated as above or below the de minimis level. Assets that exceed that threshold in value and that pose a significant potential conflict of interest must then be cured in one of the several ways available for that purpose.

The proscriptions on post-employment conduct by former presidential appointees should cease to be criminal statutes and be enforced instead through a regulatory process managed by the Office of Government Ethics.

The Ethics in Government Act of 1978 significantly broadened restrictions on the behavior of former presidential appointees. These were intended to prevent revolving-door conflicts of interest in which former government employees traded on their knowledge or contacts within government to enrich themselves, undermine agency integrity, or give unfair advantage to one interest over another. In the years since 1978, these restrictions have been expanded.

These requirements are complex and difficult to implement. The difficulty results in large part from the decision to embed these restrictions in criminal statutes. The Task Force believes that compliance with the post-employment restrictions and enforcement of them can be improved by replacing the criminal statutes in which they currently reside with a regulatory process that is more flexible and less reliant on evidence of prosecutable behavior. The 1989 Ethics Reform Act (PL 101-194) began to move the ethics laws toward civil enforcement. The Task Force believes that this was a positive step, and it supports further progress in that direction.

In most cases in which post-employment conduct is in question, there is no criminal intent. Far more common is uncertainty about whether particular kinds of actions or communications are appropriate. The Task Force believes that the proper way to address these concerns is through a regulatory process staffed by experts in the Office of Government Ethics (OGE) who, when uncertainties arise, can advise former government employees and can order them to cease and desist when they trespass beyond the boundaries of acceptable behavior. OGE should be granted the statutory authority necessary to regulate these post-employment activities.

One significant advantage of this approach is that it will reduce the fears of many potential appointees who are reluctant to enter government service because they worry about the risks when they return to the private sector. They should abide by the post-employment restrictions, but they shouldn't have to worry that an innocent contact or action will result in their indictment and possible incarceration. The Task Force believes that there is a better approach that fully serves the public interest in protecting the integrity of government decisionmaking while lowering the risks to well-meaning and law-abiding former government employees.

All parties to the appointment process should agree on a single financial disclosure form and one set of general background questions.

One of the great aggravations and a principal source of delay in the current appointment process is the requirement that nominees complete several financial disclosure forms that vary widely in the ways they are construed and respond to several different sets of background questionnaires. The White House uses one set of forms, departments and agencies use another, Senate committees still another, and the FBI and OGE still others. The financial disclosure forms often request that the same information be reported in very different ways, none of which correspond directly to the way information is reported in income tax filings. The Appendixes to the Report (see page 169) provide copies of some of these reports and questionnaires and illustrates their complexity and redundancy.

Many presidential appointees are accomplished people who have been financially successful. Their finances are complicated and these multiple reporting requirements—combined with the powerful desire to avoid the potential embarrassment of misreporting or inconsistent reporting—slow the appointment process considerably. It is not uncommon for nominees to spend a month or more gathering, sorting, and reporting the information necessary to complete all these forms.

Great efficiencies could be achieved if the parties to the appointment process, all of whom have legitimate interests in these matters, were to work together to create a single financial disclosure form and a standard background questionnaire. (A recent study of judicial appointments by the Miller Center for Public Affairs at the University of Virginia came to a similar conclusion.) It may occasionally be necessary for a department or Senate committee to solicit necessary information beyond these basic filings; they may use their own supplemental forms for that purpose. But the duplication and inconsistency in reporting standard information should be largely abolished. Everyone would benefit if it were.

Each administration should establish a small interoffice coordinating group that would meet regularly to facilitate and expedite clearances and background checks for all presidential appointees, to assist them in navigating the confirmation process, and to provide them proper orientation for their new jobs.

The slow pace of the appointment process is caused in no small part by its disjointed and decentralized character. The Personnel Office performs its functions, so do the Counsel's Office, the OGE, and the FBI. Then nominations go to the Senate where many of the steps are repeated.

The Task Force proposes the establishment of a standing, interagency committee with its own staff and with liaisons from other relevant agencies to superintend the necessary background, financial, ethical, and legal clearances on all presidential appointees. This committee's work would begin after the Presidential Personnel Office had identified and the president had approved a potential nominee and that potential nominee had agreed to serve if nominated and confirmed. Where FBI full-field investigations were required, those would occur before the nomination was handed off to this committee.

The coordinating group would conduct background reviews on all candidates not subject to FBI full-field investigations, including a search of all government computer records on the candidate, reviews of questionnaires completed by candidates, and follow-up interviews when necessary with the candidate or persons knowledgeable about the candidate. The group would have authority to call on the assistance of the FBI or other investigative agencies when such assistance would be helpful.

This interoffice coordinating group should be staffed by people with ample Washington experience, who are well-versed in the details of the ethics laws and the mechanics and politics of the confirmation process, and who command wide respect. Their work would be conducted in confidence. When completed, the information gathered by this committee would go to the president who could then make a final decision on the nomination. If the president decides to nominate the candidate, all relevant information from these investigations would be forwarded to the Senate committee with jurisdiction over the appointment. The committee's media relations officer would at this point provide a dossier of information about the nominee to the press.

The interoffice coordinating group would then work closely with the nominee and his or her representatives to:

◆ complete financial disclosure forms and other questionnaires;

◆ coordinate the nominee's compliance with the ethics laws with OGE, the appropriate designated agency ethics officer (DAEO), and the Counsel to the president's office;

◆ assist nominees in working with the staffs and meeting the members of Senate committees with jurisdiction over their nominations and prepare nominees for confirmation hearings;

◆ arrange an orientation program for all new appointees focusing on the specific concerns of their agencies and their jobs, on the Washington political environment and press corps, and on the program and objectives of the president.

The Task Force believes that this new process would significantly hasten and improve the clearances and investigations that are essential to a sound appointment process. It would overcome the decentralization that now encumbers the process and minimize the tendency for it to be held hostage to the particular agendas of individual agencies. The new process would greatly reduce duplication of reporting and investigative efforts. It would identify potential problems at an earlier stage and reduce the potential for embarrassment to the president and candidates for appointment. And it would minimize the likelihood of information leakage and thus better protect the privacy of candidates for nomination early in the process.

The clearances and checks that compose the current appointment process were born out of no careful or rational design. They grew haphazardly. It is time to centralize, coordinate, and rationalize this important set of functions. The Task Force believes that this recommendation promises real improvements in the reliability, efficiency, and integrity of the appointment process.

This recommendation also aims to make the appointment and confirmation process more "user friendly" for nominees. In effect, each nominee would have the assistance, throughout the appointment process, of an ethics lawyer, a political adviser, and a press representative. One of the constant laments of people who accept presidential appointments is that they seem to be "nobody's baby" during the confirmation process. The Personnel Office usually considers its work done when a nominee has been chosen. The Counsel's office and other agencies have specific interactions with nominees but none takes responsibility for helping the nominee, in any broad sense, to confront the confirmation and clearance process. This institutional failure is manifest in the frequent reliance of many recent nominees on the pro bono assistance of old Washington hands who have graciously, but inconsistently, stepped in to advise nominees.

That isn't good enough. The appointment process has grown steadily more complicated, elongated, and politically charged in recent decades. To many nominees from the private sector, it is an utter mystery. It is essential now that someone take responsibility for guiding nominees through the entire appointment and confirmation process. The Task Force believes as well that this is the appropriate time to be orienting nominees to the tasks and responsibilities that they will face and the environment in which they will operate. The recommendations put forth here seek to assign clear responsibility for accomplishing both of those objectives.

The major-party presidential candidates should begin to plan the staffing of their administrations well in advance of the election.

One of the great and enduring weaknesses of the contemporary appointments process is its failure to put a new administration in place on time. Presidents Bush and Clinton were both in office for more than a year before all the major positions in their administrations were filled by Senate-confirmed appointees. Modern presidents all want to hit the ground running, but soon come to realize that in the early months they are running alone. No other institution in our society would tolerate so many vacancies for so long a time in senior positions.

One way to cope with that problem is for new presidents to prepare better for their personnel responsibilities. The Task Force believes that major party candidates should begin to devote some attention to this before the election, perhaps at the time they secure their party's nomination. Candidates should appoint a staff to plan, in confidence, the personnel aspects of a transition with the full support of the nominee and his or her political and policy advisers. The staff could collect information on the full scope of the president's appointment obligations, gather or create job descriptions for key positions in the administration, master the technical details of the appointment process, become acquainted with officials in the agencies like OGE that play a key role in the appointment process, and begin to develop a personnel strategy.

The political dangers in beginning to build and winnow lists of potential appointees before an election are well-known and need not consume the attention of such a staff. But the critical importance of such pre-election planning should overcome the inhibition of appearing to be presumptuous about the outcome of the election. A good deal of the preparatory work can—and should—be done before the election so that the staffing process can proceed expeditiously immediately after the winner is determined.

There is some precedent for this. A number of recent major-party candidates have undertaken limited efforts to prepare for personnel selection. Few of these have been very successful, however. The Task Force believes that planning of this sort is essential and demands much more attention and effort than it has received in the past.

SENATE CONFIRMATION PROCESS
There should be significant modification in the practice of "holds" placed on nominations by individual senators.

The Senate is a relatively informal legislative body that grants significant deference to individual members. Over the years, a practice has emerged that allows individual senators to request of the leadership that a hold be placed on a nomination in order to gather more information, to permit a senator to meet with a nominee, or for some other practical purpose. In recent years, however, holds have become more frequent and have been used not for purposes of administrative convenience but as a tactic for delaying the confirmation process in order to extract concessions from the president or other senators.

The Task Force understands that the character and traditions of the Senate sometimes justify a temporary hold on a nomination to permit full deliberation. But the Task Force does not believe that the public interest, nor the interests of a majority of the Senate, are well served by the abuses of this practice, which have become common in recent years.

The Task Force urges the Senate to review its policy on holds and to modify it in one or more ways. One option is to limit the length of a hold to a week or ten days. Another is to require that a minimum number of senators, perhaps 10 percent of the members, must request a hold before one takes affect. A third possibility is to allow any member to offer a privileged resolution on the Senate floor that could end a hold by vote of a simple majority of those present and voting.

The Task Force does not believe that the practice of holds on nominations was established to frustrate the confirmation process or allow the conduct of important government business to be held hostage by a single senator. It believes that abuses of the holds system must end, and urges the Senate to take the necessary action to accomplish that.

Confirmation debates on executive branch appointments should be granted "fast-track" status in the Senate to shield them from filibusters.

Whatever their value for other purposes, filibusters have no place in the confirmation process for executive branch nominees. The framers of the Constitution believed that presidents should be permitted to select and be held accountable for their own appointees, subject to a vote by the Senate on the fitness of those appointees for the offices to which they were nominated. The framers deliberated carefully on what the character of the Senate check should be and decided that approval by a simple majority of the Senate was adequate to serve the public interest.

The use of filibusters on confirmations radically changes the character of the confirmation process. It requires that presidents select nominees who can obtain support of a super-majority of sixty members of the Senate, not a simple majority of fifty-one. The filibuster allows a minority of forty senators to control who will or will not serve in a presidential administration. In a time of divided government—of the sort that has become normal in recent decades—the filibuster creates abundant opportunities for partisan mischief in the appointment process.

In recent years, while it has retained the filibuster rule, the Senate has come to realize that there are some areas of its jurisdiction from which filibusters should be excluded. Filibusters are not now permitted in the process used to close military bases. Important trade agreements are often beyond the reach of the filibuster. The annual budget resolution and ensuing reconciliation legislation cannot be filibustered. Before the Supreme Court struck down the use of legislative vetoes, many proposals that came to the Senate were not subject to filibusters.

The Task Force believes that presidential nominations should proceed on a "fast track" in the Senate. They should be scheduled for floor vote within fifteen legislative days after being reported out of committee, and they should receive a shield from the filibuster and other forms of procedural delay. The Task Force would exempt judicial nominations from these requirements. Because they involve life tenure in a third branch of government and because judicial vacancies are significantly different in character from administrative vacancies, Senate deliberation does and should proceed more slowly.

The efficient conduct of government business cannot occur when presidents—and even majorities in the Senate—are held hostage by determined minorities employing the filibuster rule. The Senate has an important constitutional role in the appointment process. The Task Force believes it should play that role fully and carefully. But the Task Force also believes that it should do so by majority rule. Any other practice is deeply threatening to the framers' wise intent and to good government.

It is equally important that Senate committees not unduly delay confirmation decisions, especially by using appointments as bargaining chips in policy disagreements between committee members and the president. The Task Force recognizes the long-standing deference the Senate affords its committees in all matters, but must also note that long delays in committee action leave the affected nominee and the departments and agencies awaiting their leadership in highly uncomfortable limbo, undermine the president's ability to govern, and discourage other talented individuals from accepting future offers of appointment.

Confirmation hearings should be waived for noncontroversial appointments to lower-level positions.

For most of our history, the Senate did not hold public hearings on nominations to any office. When the practice began, it spread quickly and has now come to consume a good deal of the time of some Senate committees and to produce a good deal of unnecessary anxiety among nominees. The American people are most familiar with the few extraordinary, and often hostile, confirmation hearings that prick the public consciousness. Those, however, are clearly exceptional. Most confirmation hearings are routine, pro forma, and short. They produce little valuable information and often seem simply unnecessary. Scheduling of hearings is often a significant source of delay in the confirmation process. Committee staff must frequently scramble on the day of the hearing to find a single senator willing to chair the proceeding.

The Task Force urges the Senate to raise the threshold for confirmation hearings, limiting them only to those offices or nominations in which individual senators have genuine interest or concern. For some years, the Senate has followed the practice on military promotions of publishing the list of candidates and holding them for a limited time. During that time, any senator can demand a hearing on a particular nominee. Absent such demands, no formal hearings are held. The Task Force believes that this practice should be applied more widely to include nearly all nominations. Where no senators express significant interest in or concern regarding a nomination, the Task Force believes that the waiver of confirmation hearings will be of value in expediting the confirmation process.

Senate committees should conduct executive sessions for examination of certain personal matters or criticisms of nominees based on questionable evidence.

The Senate has every right, indeed is obligated, to inquire into personal matters or questions of character that might affect a nominee's performance in office. It also has a duty to examine criticisms of, or complaints about, a nominee.

The Task Force believes, however, that it is most often appropriate, especially in the early stages of a hearing, to explore these sensitive issues in executive session. This approach would both protect the
appropriate privacy of the nominee and maintain the integrity of the
confirmation process from charges of unfairness or political bias.
Matters initially explored in executive session may later warrant discussion in open session. But fairness requires that nominees be considered innocent and worthy of appointment until proper evidence
demonstrates otherwise.

Public discussions of personal matters and attacks on the character of some recent nominees have had a chilling effect on the
appointment process. Too many potential appointees these days
decline nomination because they do not wish to be subjected to the
kinds of abusive confirmation hearings they've watched on television.
The Task Force believes that the Senate has an obligation to exercise
extreme caution in subjecting nominees to potential abuse. Broader
use of executive sessions is one way to accomplish that.

A CALL FOR GREATER CIVILITY

One of the greatest threats to the historically high quality of public
servants in America is the growing reluctance of talented individuals to accept presidential appointments. Throughout its deliberations,
the Task Force has heard story after story of highly qualified individuals who have declined to accept presidential appointments because
they did not want to be subjected to the intense and sometimes irrelevant scrutiny or to the personal abuse that have become increasingly common in the appointment process. "It's not worth it" is the
refrain born of this reluctance. Our nation suffers gravely when so
many good people find the prospect of entering public service so
forbidding.

Change in the character of the appointment process is the
responsibility of everyone who participates in it or reports on it.
Presidents should be more cautious about the practice of floating
"trial balloons"—suggesting names of potential nominees as a way of
determining what kind of opposition they might draw if nominated.
Members of presidential administrations must cease the leaks
designed to undermine internal candidates they oppose. People and
groups who disagree with a nominee's policy views must frame their
opposition to the nominee in policy, not personal, terms. Senators
and their staffs must step up their efforts to ensure the integrity of the

confirmation process by redoubling their efforts to prevent malicious leaks of information or rumor and by making every effort to keep the focus of their attention on the policy views and professional qualifications of nominees. Reporters and editors should take great care to report only reliable and relevant information about nominees and to avoid personal information about individuals that is unverified or irrelevant to their nominations.

To accomplish these changes will be no simple task. Appointments matter because they deeply affect the course of public policy. They are always inviting political targets. Appointments are also "good copy." Unlike much that goes on in government, they are relatively easy to comprehend. Stories about them can focus on personal drama rather than the complexities of public policy. The Task Force recognizes the temptations and political logic that have led to recent excesses in the politics and media coverage of the appointment process. It also recognizes that thoughtful people reasonably disagree about appropriate topics for investigation, discussion, and news coverage in this process. There is no current consensus on where the public's right to know ends and an appointee's right to privacy begins.

These perplexities make it all the more important for people who work in, try to influence the outcomes of, or report on the appointment process to take special cognizance of their responsibility to exercise caution. Individuals willing to serve the public as presidential appointees deserve some protection from unnecessary or unfounded attacks on their integrity, character, or prior life history.

The Task Force believes that candidates for presidential appointments are entitled to a zone of privacy and that all discussions of individual nominees should be subject to the careful discipline of relevance and reliability. Beyond essential questions of policy and philosophy, the appointment process should focus only on the personal characteristics and qualifications of the nominee that are relevant to the position for which they are nominated and be based on reliable evidence.

But even this approach is no substitute for caution and concern for the public interest. In the appointment process, winning a battle often does contribute to losing the war. When an appointment is killed by abusive and excessive personal attacks, or even if it succeeds in spite of them, good people around the country take note. Their reluctance to subject themselves to a protracted ordeal is solidified. We all suffer as a consequence. And so all of us must share the responsibility for restoring civilized discourse and procedural integrity to the appointment process. If we do not, the pool of talented and creative Americans who are willing to serve their country as presidential appointees will continue to shrink.

DISSENT AND COMMENTS

DISSENT

CONSTANCE HORNER

I do not agree with the Report's premise that there is or should be an inviolable "zone of privacy" for nominees, such that some areas of inquiry are ruled out-of-bounds in the nomination and confirmation process. From time to time, participants in the process have abused and maligned potential appointees. However, responsible inquiries into character have also identified serious evidence of unfitness to serve. Moreover, in many controversial arenas, there is no national consensus as to what constitutes good character. One person's foible—or even virtue—is another's mortal sin. One person's private choice is another person's public policy issue. These kinds of differences are best resolved by the discipline of the democratic process. Suppression of controversial deliberations by the decision of people in power only embitters citizens who would challenge those people and their values. It is more unwholesome to engage in such suppression than to lose potential nominees deterred by fear of public scrutiny.

Civility is important. Therefore, abusive, dishonest attackers should be confronted and their own political and professional reputations damaged. But a president's choice of nominee and a Congress's ratification of that choice reflect their values and thus ought to be subjected to political evaluation, as are other decisions.

Some think of appointees as morally neutral technicians whose personal probity and embodiment of the community's standards are irrelevant to the job at hand. But as far back as George Washington, who called "fitness of character" the salient factor in the choice of appointees, Americans have looked to the president's appointees not only to get a job done, but to lead the nation by edifying example. In a nation of more than 250 million people, there are sufficient numbers of talented and experienced people of high moral standards available for public service. We ought not either to define our expectations down or evade the real and serious conflicts entailed in defining those expectations.

On another subject, many of the Report's recommendations propose to shift some power over appointments from the Congress to the president. These recommendations are, in my view, sound on the merits. However, it is worth noting that support for such a shift among bodies such as those advising on this Report strengthened just as the Republican party gained control of the Congress for the first time in forty years. Thus, if a recommendation for a shift of power between the branches is not hospitably received by the new Congress—which knows the institutional influence of its predecessors—it should come as no surprise.

COMMENT

ARNIE MILLER

I support the important procedural changes recommended by the Task Force. To derive full potential from its human resources, however, the federal government requires a strategy and a focus even broader than the one laid out in this Report. Modern corporations devote extraordinary attention to the full development and wise deployment of their employees. The federal government must do so as well.

Presidents, especially, must adopt many of the strategies used by major corporations and other large organizations to develop better their human resources. Obviously, there are differences between a national administration and a private company or organization. But there are important parallels as well, and the federal government can learn much about recruiting and retraining excellent people from the experiences of others.

♦ Succession planning and career planning should be instituted even at the highest levels of the federal government. Particularly talented people should be identified and their careers tracked and carefully cultivated.

♦ Steps should be taken to provide for some continuity in order to avoid having to "start from scratch." A talented bank of genuinely outstanding people available for service should be developed, maintained, and updated by the Presidential Personnel Office. When a party is out of power, this function might be performed by its national committee or some other entity established for this purpose.

◆   Reducing turnover should be an explicit objective of federal
    human resources policy. The average tenure of an assistant sec-
    retary has now fallen below two years. Appointees should be
    expected to commit to serve for a full four-year term. Not only
    would this improve the management of departments and agen-
    cies and the ability of presidents to implement their agendas, it
    would also substantially reduce the number of appointments in
    the course of a president's term and the attendant burdens on
    the entire appointments process.

◆   Orientation and training programs should begin before
    appointees are confirmed and continue throughout their tenure.

◆   A range of strategies should be employed to help appointees and
    their families feel more a part of an administration. Too many
    now feel isolated in their agencies and apart from the action.
    Such strategies might include frequent interdepartmental task
    forces convened at the White House to formulate and/or exe-
    cute policy; periodic briefings for appointees and their spouses by
    senior administration officials on overall political and policy
    objectives; photo opportunities with the president and the vice
    president; and social events at the White House for families of
    appointees.

These suggestions are illustrative. More thought and attention needs
to be paid to how national administrations manage and cultivate their
human resources.

COMMENT

PAUL A. VOLCKER

The Report lays out an ambitious and constructive program for improving the appointment process, much of which, unfortunately, is sure to encounter political and administrative resistance.

That is true of what I regard as by far the most important single recommendation: that "the number of presidential appointments should be substantially reduced, perhaps by approximately a third of the current total." The recommendation parallels a proposal by the National Commission on the Public Service six years ago, which was in turn based upon scholarly research and the broad experience of commission members with elective, appointive, and career public service.

Contrary to the impression of many, multiplication of the numbers of "political" appointees over the years impedes rather than enhances the ability of a president to direct and control his administration. This Report amply documents the hazards of appointment and confirmation that have become a barrier to service to many potential appointees. Moreover, those who are willing and able to serve typically are in office for two years or less.

With three thousand or so appointees, the allure of subsidiary jobs for high quality candidates and the ability of a president to insist upon and enforce demanding standards are dissipated. Inevitably, many of those actively interested in appointment have personal agendas—political or private—that may be at odds with those of the president. And, perhaps most insidiously, we end up with too many "political" layers, at the expense of developing and maintaining energetic and qualified career professionals.

Instead of efficiently advancing coherent administration programs, too often the end result of the process is infighting and inef-
fectiveness. But it is also true that some of the pressure for more
political appointees is a response to the similar proliferation of congressional staff generating politically charged proposals and inquiries
that must be dealt with in a politically sensitive way. Recent efforts by
the Congress to reduce its own staff are thus a logical complement to
the Task Force proposal.

Finally, if the number of political appointees both on "the Hill"
and "downtown" is not reduced, far more attention needs to be paid
to encouraging the kind of responsive, energetic, professional and
ethical career service this country needs. That was not the charge of
this Task Force, but it seems to me the logical corollary of what we
have proposed.

BACKGROUND PAPERS

THE PRESIDENTIAL APPOINTMENT PROCESS:
HISTORICAL DEVELOPMENT, CONTEMPORARY OPERATIONS, CURRENT ISSUES

G. CALVIN MACKENZIE

PREFACE

The modern presidential appointment process barely resembles its constitutional design or intent. In fact, it differs dramatically from the way presidents made appointments as recently as the late 1940s. There are more jobs to fill than ever before, and many of those positions involve complex and technical duties. The appointment process is much more formal and structured. It takes longer, often many months longer, to fill an appointive position than it did just a few decades ago. And the process is more visible and more consistently contentious than ever.

These changes raise hard questions about the burden the modern appointment process places on the president. They raise even harder questions about the impact of the process on the appointees who must endure it in order to serve their country in positions of great responsibility.

This paper examines the historical development of the modern appointment process and explains its current operations. It then takes a close look at the transition experience of President Bill Clinton. It concludes by identifying and exploring several persistent and troubling issues emerging from the ways in which presidents now recruit and review their appointees and the manner in which the Senate exercises its responsibility to advise and give consent on their nominations.

1

THE DEVELOPMENT OF THE CONTEMPORARY APPOINTMENT PROCESS

Staffing a presidential administration was easier in George Washington's time than it is now. The government was tiny by contemporary standards, and most of the leading politicians were well known to the president. Washington, for example, was able to fill the handful of top posts in his administration with political allies and close personal friends. Thomas Jefferson, Henry Knox, Edmund Randolph, and Alexander Hamilton filled the cabinet slots; Thomas Pinckney was appointed ambassador to Great Britain and Gouverneur Morris to France; John Jay became the first chief justice.

This practice of filling appointments with personal acquaintances and close political allies remained in place until Andrew Jackson was elected in 1828. Jackson's election marked the beginning of a new kind of politics in the United States, one rooted in broad-based, national political parties. Success in presidential elections had come to require the mobilization of rank and file voters all across a country that was rapidly moving westward. To sustain growing party organizations, presidents began to use appointments as patronage, as rewards for political efforts on their behalf.

For most of the century that followed, the patronage system remained in place. The creation of a national civil service in 1883 slowly changed the process of filling the lower-level positions in the government; but, with very few exceptions, senior positions—the government's top executives—continued to be filled by party leaders and loyalists.

Cabinet-making in this period became a political balancing act. Fitness for appointment had little to do with managerial skills or policy views or even loyalty to the president. It had much to do with constructing and sustaining party coalitions. Because the White House and the Congress were almost always controlled by the same political party and because vast and sinewy webs of partisanship connected leaders in both branches, the appointment process was largely a partisan operation. It was managed outside the White House, and the dominant determinants of fitness for appointment were a record of effort on the party's behalf and the sponsorship of a powerful party leader. With but few exceptions, presidents appointed no one who was not sent to them by party leaders.

Woodrow Wilson's first cabinet, for example, was emblematic of cabinets of the time. It included William Jennings Bryan as secretary of state and Josephus Daniels as secretary of the navy. Neither was a close acquaintance. Neither had demonstrated notable competence concerning the substantive issues for which their departments were responsible. Both, in fact, represented wings of the Democratic party different from Wilson's. Their presence in his cabinet was the product almost entirely of partisan, not managerial, calculations.

RECRUITING FOR THE PRESIDENT:
THE CHANGE AT MID-CENTURY

Only with the emergence of the New Deal did the recruiting demands of the government begin to outgrow the supply capacity of the political party organizations. The New Deal and then World War II produced two very significant changes in American political life. First, they enlarged the size and scope of the federal government. Federal expenditures grew from $3.1 billion in 1930 to $95.2 billion in 1945. And federal civilian employment grew about as rapidly, from 601,000 in 1930 to 3,816,000 in 1945.[1] The consequence for leadership was clear: running the federal government became an enormous and complex operation, requiring executive talent of the highest quality. It could no longer be given over to party hacks.

A second consequence of the third and fourth decades of this century was a vast centralization of public policy in the government in

Washington. Before the New Deal, Americans did not look to Washington for solutions to many of their problems. The government in those days did not provide aid to education, run a national pension system, provide health care for the elderly, fund the national highway system, regulate financial markets, shoot rockets into space, or serve as democracy's policeman around the world. It does all of those things and many more today, and it spends one and a half trillion dollars each year doing them. The national government has become more important, and, as it has, Americans have come to expect higher and higher levels of performance from the institutions on which they increasingly rely—and for whose services they pay dearly.

Those demands are exacerbated by the growing technological character of much of what government does. Before 1930, government's scientific responsibilities rarely included much more than building some roads and canals, registering patents, conducting some agricultural experiments, and improving weaponry for the army and navy. As we approach the end of the twentieth century, the national government is perched on the cutting edge of virtually every scientific discipline and technological problem: AIDS research, astrophysics, genetic engineering, food and drug regulation, and on and on. A recent study by the National Academy of Sciences noted the impact of this change on presidential recruiting.

> The government of the United States today is deeply involved in important policy areas that have significant scientific and technical components. The science and technology activities of the federal government are vitally important for economic productivity and technological competitiveness, national security, an improved environment, better health, and many other purposes. As scientific and technological knowledge continues to expand at a rapid rate, the government needs ever greater capacity to formulate, carry out, and monitor S&T policies and programs and their effects. The need for highly competent and dedicated scientists, engineers, and other experts in top policy and management positions in the federal government has never been greater.[2]

So the government is not only larger—with some 5 million employees—but more deeply involved in all of the complexities of modern life. And it has become the real center of American society:

spending a quarter of our gross national product, determining social
priorities, redistributing economic costs and benefits, regulating virtually every aspect of our lives. As the federal government has grown in
size and responsibility, the number of presidential appointees has
expanded.

That expansion, as Paul Light has recently noted, is the product
of the "thickening and widening" of the federal government. There
are more departments and agencies than there were a few decades
ago and they administer more programs. New appointive positions
have been created to manage those new departments and agencies. At
the same time, federal government administration has grown increasingly top heavy. Departments have added more under secretaries,
assistant secretaries, deputy assistant secretaries, associate deputy assistant secretaries, and so on. Table 1.1 indicates the magnitude of
recent expansion in the top levels of the cabinet departments.

In a government with 5 million employees, the number of presidential appointees is still relatively small. But those appointees sit at
the top of every organization chart, and their coming and going is the
dominant rhythm of public management in Washington. The number
of presidential appointees changes constantly; Table 1.2 provides a
recent accounting.

TABLE 1.1
GROWTH IN TOP-LEVEL EXECUTIVE BRANCH POSITIONS
1960–1993

TITLE	No. in Kennedy Administration	No. in Clinton Administration
Secretary	10	14
Deputy Secretary	6	21
Under Secretary	15	32
Assistant Secretary	87	212
Deputy Assistant Secretary	78	507
Total	196	786

Source: Paul C. Light, Thickening Government: Why It Matters, How It Happened, and
What To Do about It (Washington, D.C.: The Brookings Institution, 1995), pp. 190–92.

TABLE 1.2
PRESIDENTIAL APPOINTEES BY ORGANIZATIONAL
LOCATION AND TYPE, 1992

DEPARTMENT	PAS* Full-Time	PAS Part-Time	PA* Full-Time	PA Part-Time
State	64	36	5	97
Ambassadors	165			
Treasury	32			4
Defense	51	13		3
Justice	48	2		6
U.S. Marshals	93			
U.S. Attorneys	94			
Interior	19			1
Agriculture	17	7		7
Commerce	32		1	
Labor	19			5
HHS	20		4	18
HUD	14	1		
Transportation	19	5		
Energy	25			
Education	19	15		38
Veterans	15			
Subtotal	746	79	10	179
Independent Agencies and Commissions	269	426	14	1,405
White House Staff Appointed by President				338
Total	1,015	505	362	1,584
(Federal Judges	956)			
Grand Total, Executive Branch	3,466			

*PAS = Presidential appointment requiring Senate confirmation.
*PA = Presidential appointment not requiring Senate confirmation.

Source: Office of the Executive Clerk, the White House.

An additional, powerful force in elevating the importance of the presidential appointment process has been the pattern of declining tenure among presidential appointees. Once appointed, they don't stay in office for very long. High turnover has reached epidemic proportions in the federal government. As Figure 1.1 illustrates, the average appointee now stays on the job for only slightly longer than two years; almost a third have a tenure shorter than eighteen months. Given the political and substantive complexity of the jobs they hold, this high turnover directly affects the quality of the leadership and management presidential appointees provide to the presidents they serve. Teams of administrators are constantly changing and readjusting to new members. Persistence in pursuit of policy objectives is increasingly rare as administrative agendas and priorities change almost constantly.

APPOINTEE RECRUITMENT:
MODERNIZATION BEGINS

As important changes occurred in the character of government and the role and number of presidential appointees in the middle decades of the twentieth century, the executive recruitment process was also undergoing a metamorphosis. Faced with the need to appoint a steadily growing number of appointees and to recruit individuals with significant talents and substantive expertise, presidents began to devise more systematic procedures for recruiting executives and slowly came to realize the value of placing this function in the hands of specialists.

Dwight D. Eisenhower was the first to respond to a modern president's need for centralized control over executive branch personnel by seeking to construct procedures and organizational structures to serve that objective. The position of Special Assistant for Personnel Management was created in 1958, and the first elements of a systematic recruitment operation were put in place. But this occurred late in the Eisenhower presidency and never established a strong enough pattern to become a precedent for subsequent administrations.

The momentum toward centralized presidential control of the appointment process and away from reliance on party patronage accelerated in the Kennedy and Johnson administrations. John F. Kennedy had won the presidential nomination by setting up his own organization and capturing his party. His was not a life of deeply committed partisanship nor did he grant the Democratic party organization much credit for his narrow victory in the 1960 election. So Kennedy felt little compulsion to staff his administration with party

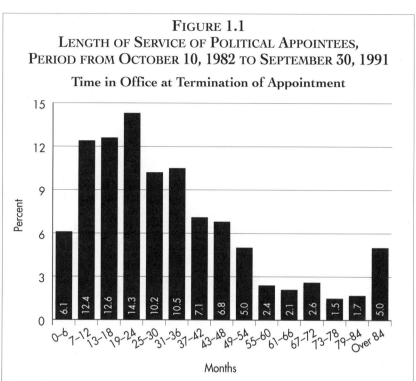

FIGURE 1.1
LENGTH OF SERVICE OF POLITICAL APPOINTEES,
PERIOD FROM OCTOBER 10, 1982 TO SEPTEMBER 30, 1991

Time in Office at Termination of Appointment

Source: Drawn from information provided by General Accounting Office, *Political Appointees: Turnover Rates in Executive Schedule Positions Requiring Senate Confirmation,* GGD–94–115FS, April 21, 1994.

loyalists to whom he might have had any debt or obligation. From the very start, he and his staff operated their own personnel recruitment operation. In several important ways, they invented the modern appointment process.

That first personnel staff was small, with just three professionals and three secretaries. None of its members was a professional executive recruiter, but its operational leader was Dan H. Fenn, Jr., who had been on the faculty at the Harvard Business School and had a broad understanding of professional methods of executive search. Fenn's first acquaintance with the recruitment methods then in place in government left him shocked at their lack of sophistication. It was, wrote Fenn, a "BOGSAT" system: a Bunch Of Guys Sitting Around a Table, asking one another "Whom do you know?" It emphasized the screening of applicants rather than aggressive recruiting, and Fenn thought it a limited and unsatisfactory method for filling the country's most important political offices.[3]

Fenn's major contribution was to cultivate the notion that a president's personnel needs could only be met by active and aggressive recruiting. No modern president could satisfactorily rely on political parties or the applications and nominations that came in over the transom to meet executive personnel needs. The president needed a staff of able recruiters to search for the best people in the country and recruit them to fill executive positions in government. "We were not in the patronage business," Fenn later said. "We were able to hold pretty much to the process of recruiting presidential appointees."[4]

After Kennedy's assassination, Lyndon Johnson continued the practice of operating a proactive White House Personnel Office. He designated John Macy, then chairman of the Civil Service Commission, to handle presidential appointments as well. Under Macy, the Personnel Office grew in size and sophistication, even employing computers to maintain records on thousands of potential appointees.

During both the Kennedy and Johnson presidencies, the White House Personnel Office worked with the Democratic National Committee, in varying degrees of cooperation. But the participation of the party was clearly subsidiary. Most of the time, the National Committee's role was to determine that candidates for appointment selected by the White House would not incur the opposition of party leaders in their home states. The White House also conducted checks with home state Democratic senators and members of Congress to avoid opposition from them. But, as Dan Fenn said, "The kind of people we were looking for weren't the kind of people who were active in party activities."[5] While party officials were a steady source of suggestions of potential nominees, genuine control over personnel selection had shifted to the White House.

THE 1970S AND 1980S:
INSTITUTIONALIZATION OF PRESIDENTIAL PERSONNEL

The movement to professionalize the executive recruitment process reached new levels of sophistication and success in the administration of Richard Nixon and in those that followed. Nixon himself never had much interest in personnel selection, but the people to whom he delegated that task tended to be experienced professional managers, many of them with business backgrounds, who saw personnel selection as a critical ingredient in efforts to establish control over the executive branch.

After 1969, the White House Personnel Office (later called the Presidential Personnel Office) became an important component of the president's staff structure and grew in size. It now routinely employs more than thirty people, and often swells to a hundred at particularly busy times. Appointment procedures have been systematized and routinized. Computers play an important role in tracking the progress of appointments. And clearances with leaders of the president's party, with relevant members of Congress, with officials in the agency to which an appointment is to be made, and with policy specialists in the administration are regular features of almost every appointment decision.

The clearance process has grown more elaborate for two reasons. One is simply that there are more checkpoints than ever before: more White House staff aides, more interest groups, and more congressional committees and subcommittees. The drama of any single appointment has been lengthened and enlarged by the growing cast of actors involved. The second reason is related to the first. Modern presidents have all had their share of appointment controversies. Those controversies are distracting and painful—for the president as well as the nominee. The clearance process is now used as an early warning system, to detect potential trouble and to either neutralize it in advance or avoid appointments that are going to be troublesome. The elaborate thickness of the contemporary appointment process reflects, more than anything, this kind of defensiveness: a desire to identify trouble in advance and navigate around it.

But the most important characteristic of the modern appointment process, and the one that most clearly marks the difference between the old and the new, has been the creation of a genuine and aggressive recruitment or outreach capability within the White House staff. This started during the Kennedy years, but only on a small scale. Ralph Dungan, a personnel aide to Kennedy, noted of this effort, "It was so crude, I am almost embarrassed to talk about it. But it was at least a step toward systematizing the headhunter process."[6]

The real turning point came in 1970. After nearly two years in office, Richard Nixon's top aides were unhappy with the way his administration was handling its staffing functions. Too many appointments were being filled by people who had not been fully cleared by the White House and whose loyalty to Nixon's programs was inadequate. Nixon's frustrations with bureaucratic bungling and insubordination had grown steadily through the early years of his presidency.

As he said in a pungent comment to John Ehrlichman, recorded on the White House tapes, "We have no discipline in this bureaucracy. We never fire anybody. We never reprimand anybody. We always promote the sons-of-bitches that kick us in the ass."

Frederic V. Malek, who had gained favorable attention at the White House for the management skills he had demonstrated in his work at the Department of Health, Education, and Welfare, was assigned the task of analyzing the White House personnel function. He found much to criticize and wrote a report calling for the creation of a centralized White House Personnel Operation and significant changes in recruitment procedures. Malek later wrote of the critical importance of sound appointment decisions to a president's success:

> In today's government, the Cabinet and the White House staff exert powerful influence on the direction of an administration, and most decisions that are credited to a President are actually made at the staff level with only pro forma approval from the President. The people around the chief executive are the ones who actually run the agencies, sift through the issues, identify the problems, and present analyses and recommendations for the chief's decision. It is they who give shape to the administration's governing strategy and transform vague party platforms to hard policies and legislative proposals.[7]

When Malek's report was completed, H. R. Haldeman designated him to head the new personnel office he had recommended, and Malek set up the first full-fledged, professional White House recruitment effort. He hired E. Pendleton James from the firm of Heidrick and Struggles and a group of other executive search professionals to lend their skills to the task of identifying and recruiting new talent for the Nixon administration.

The problem, as Malek phrased it, was the common one in recruiting: "Typically, the kind of person we want is not looking for a government job. He's happy where he is, doing something constructive, making more money than we can offer him and has great advancement potential. Many are in their mid-30's and earning six figure incomes."[8] As leadership jobs in government were becoming more demanding and difficult, as the political environment grew more hostile, as the gap between government and private sector salaries was broadening, as a changing society produced more dual career couples and family pressures, finding and recruiting the talent necessary to run a complex modern government became an ever-greater challenge.

Thus, as the president's appointment responsibilities expanded, the task was to build a staff structure in the White House that could meet the continuing need for able appointees to fill demanding positions in the executive branch. The paraphernalia of that structure—professional recruiters, systematized procedures, computer data banks, and linkages with other power centers—emerged in the 1960s and matured through the two decades that followed. They have endured and are now a fundamental element of the institutionalized presidency.

2

THE APPOINTMENT PROCESS
IN OPERATION

No two administrations conduct the appointment process in exactly the same way. But practices and requirements regarding recruitment, clearances, and confirmation have developed over time that now structure every president's appointment routines.

RECRUITMENT

For all of the elaboration and sophistication of the appointment process that has occurred over recent decades, the identification and recruitment of appointees remains decidedly unsystematic. American political parties do not have shadow cabinets or governments in exile. Americans vote for a new president with no certain knowledge of who will staff that president's administration. Often presidential candidates themselves have only the foggiest notions about whom they'll choose to govern with them.

Recruitment of an administration is thus only slightly structured chaos. No sooner has the last vote been cast than the resumes start flowing. During the early Clinton transition they flowed at the rate of 15,000 a week. They don't just arrive in the mail. They come pouring out of fax machines. They are hand delivered by powerful sponsors looking for jobs for favorite staff members, constituents, old allies, or brothers-in-law. There is a good deal of entrepreneurial activity during this period by people seeking a clever new angle of assault on the small group of people who actually help presidents select their appointees. One recent presidential personnel aide tells of parking his car in the garage under his Washington apartment building late at night. As he walked toward the elevator, a figure in a trench coat approached him from out of the shadows. The figure walked up to the aide, grabbed his lapel, stuck a folded resume in his coat pocket, pivoted, and walked away without saying a word. No job ensued, but the personnel aide started parking closer to the elevator at night.

Constructing an administration is part political balancing act, part finding jobs for old friends, and part careful searching. Every appointment is a little drama of its own, and no decision calculus applies to any two positions in the same way. Bill Clinton came to Washington with a broad circle of acquaintances with leadership and policy credentials. So, too, did Hillary Rodham Clinton. Many appointees were drawn from this group during the Clinton transition. Other presidents lack a resource this large and are forced to staff their administrations with people not so well known to them, often not known to them at all. Even Richard Nixon, for example, despite more than two decades of national political experience at the time of his election, staffed his administration largely with people who were strangers to him at the time of their appointments.

Typically, and especially at the beginning of a new administration, recruitment occurs in several ways simultaneously. The president and his handful of longtime and trusted aides concentrate on the most important positions and generally fill them with people they know well or whose reputations will add something important to the administration. At the same time, a personnel operation is at work identifying and sorting strongly qualified candidates for second- and third-tier positions. Meanwhile, leaders of the president's campaign are lobbying for the appointment of people who worked hard to get the president elected. Surrounding these spheres of activity are members of Congress, interest group leaders, old acquaintances of the president, and many others seeking to influence these choices for self-interested reasons. E. Pendleton James, who worked in the Nixon personnel office and later directed personnel selection during the Reagan transition likened the process to "drinking from a fire hydrant."[1] The pressures on presidents and their recruiters are relentless.

Communication among the various participants in appointee recruitment is often inexact, especially in the immediate aftermath of the election before appointment routines have been put in place. Dan Fenn recalled from his days as a recruiter for President Kennedy:

> I remember we did an awful lot of work on Abe Ribicoff's successor at HEW—turned out to be [Anthony J.] Celebreze. Ralph [Dungan] and I were working on this and we had a marvelous list of people. I went to bring it in to the President one day. I got there a little bit late. Ralph had gone in already and I said, "Kenny, can I go in?" He said, "What have you got?" I said, "HEW." He said, "Oh, we settled that two months ago."[2]

Fenn was not the last presidential personnel aide to have such an experience.

Once structured procedures begin to take hold, the Presidential Personnel Office superintends the recruitment of the vast majority of an administration's appointees. It begins by identifying a vacancy that needs to be filled and determining the specific requirements—both formal and informal—of the job. Then names of potential candidates are gathered. The president may have a candidate in mind. The relevant department or agency head will often want to fill the position with someone of his or her choosing. Other people close to the president may have candidates in mind as well. In recent years, for example, White House chiefs of staff have sometimes played highly influential roles in selecting appointees. Often, as well, interesting candidates will turn up through the recruitment processes of the personnel office.

As names of potential candidates accumulate, discussions intensify between the White House and department or agency head. In some administrations, like Nixon's and Carter's, appointees were given wide latitude in selecting their subordinates—though, it should be noted, both presidents later came to regret this early decision. With other presidents, Reagan most notably, control over appointments has been closely held in the White House. In all administrations, however, some degree of negotiation between the White House and the relevant department precedes almost every appointment.

These discussions usually yield a short list of candidates or, sometimes, consensus on a single candidate. This is reported to the president who either accedes to the recommendation offered by the personnel office, chooses among the choices provided, seeks more information, or rejects all the candidates and asks for others. Presidents vary widely in the extent of their personal involvement in appointment decisions. Eisenhower and Nixon were probably the least involved of the post-war presidents. Johnson, Ford, and Clinton played the largest roles in making these choices.

Either just before or just after the president has selected a candidate for the nomination, senior members of the White House staff are given an opportunity to comment. The clearance list varies with the position. Where a nominee will be involved in foreign or economic policymaking, for example, the national security adviser or chair of the Council of Economic Advisers will be asked for comments. In general, this process of "staffing around" is intended to uncover potential land mines, to make sure that the nomination will not harm or embarrass the president politically or substantively. Nearly all senior nominations are subjected to this process; in some administrations, Reagan's most notably, even lower-level appointments not requiring Senate confirmation were often staffed around. Nominations that survive this internal process then go forward through a set of increasingly formal clearances.

CLEARANCES

The timing of the clearances described below varies widely. Some may occur before a candidate is selected as the nominee for a position; others may unfold after the nomination has been announced. Some begin on one side of the announcement and continue on the other. In some cases, the clearances and investigations may take a half year or more to complete; six months, in fact, is widely regarded as the norm. But in a rush, the processing of a nomination can move at light speed. Bobby Inman withdrew his nomination as secretary of defense on January 18, 1994. Six days later, President Clinton announced William Perry as the new nominee. Perry was confirmed and sworn in on February 3rd. The process moved with similar speed to confirm Richard Cheney as secretary of defense after the Senate defeated John Tower's nomination to that position in early 1989.

CONGRESSIONAL CLEARANCE

The Congress is a prominent feature on any president's political landscape, and the selection of appointees is an important component of executive-legislative relations. Sensitivity to concerns that congressional leaders might have in the appointment process can often strengthen the president's working relations with them. Hence routine efforts are made to inform members of Congress of the progress of a search and to allow them opportunities to express their reactions to the candidates under consideration. Among those most often consulted on appointments are the leaders of the president's party in the House and Senate, the senators and influential representatives from the candidate's home state who are members of the president's party, and the leaders of the committees and subcommittees with jurisdiction over the agency in which the nominee will serve.

Most of the contact with members of Congress on appointment matters is handled by the White House congressional relations staff, the people who work with Congress every day. Members of Congress generally recognize that the appointment power belongs to the president and that by "clearing" a nomination with them, the White House is not offering an opportunity for a veto, only for a reaction. This is essentially a process of information exchange and, except in a few cases, not much more. It would normally require a major objection, strongly expressed by a member of Congress, to stop a nomination at this point. In reality, the vast majority of congressional clearances result in pro forma approval.

Congressional clearances are not always successful in ferreting out or measuring potential opposition. Late in 1993, for example, President Clinton's intention to nominate John Payton as assistant attorney general for civil rights was torpedoed by opposition from the Congressional Black Caucus after Payton held troubling interviews with members of the Caucus.

FBI FULL-FIELD INVESTIGATION

The full-field investigation is a comprehensive inquiry designed to determine whether there is information that might disqualify a candidate from holding high office or that might embarrass the president were it to become public. The requirement for a full-field investigation on all candidates for presidential appointment originated with President Dwight Eisenhower's Executive Order 10450 in 1953.

Most full-field investigations are conducted by a unit of the Criminal Investigation Division of the FBI that handles "special inquiries" from the White House, the "SPIN Unit." The investigations focus on the candidate's character, associations, reputation, and loyalty. The background investigation covers the candidate's entire adult life with emphasis on the recent past. Those interviewed by FBI agents are told that the candidate is being considered for a government position, but the position is not identified. In some cases, the FBI may not know what the position is.

At the outset of the investigation, the candidate fills out several FBI forms and is interviewed to ensure that information supplied on the forms is complete and accurate. The interview also seeks to identify any information known to the candidate that could have a bearing on his or her suitability for government employment and/or access to classified information. The FBI field office in the region of current residence and/or employment will normally conduct the interview.

The investigation focuses on several areas. The candidate's educational record is examined to verify that he or she did indeed earn the academic degrees claimed. The neighborhoods in which the candidate has lived in the past five years will be visited, and present or former neighbors interviewed. The agents verify the candidate's employment records and often interview business associates. If the candidate's business had contact with, or was regulated by, a government agency, the agency's files may be checked for any record of problems. Inquiries are also made of any government agency for which the candidate has worked; central government data files, civilian and military, are also checked. Certain financial records of the candidate will be checked for bad debts or financial improprieties.

Medical records pertaining to a candidate's physical well-being are not routinely examined by the FBI. However, mental health records are usually reviewed when it is established that a candidate has undergone psychiatric or psychological counseling or treatment. If these records need to be reviewed, the candidate will be asked to sign a special release form granting access to pertinent files.

Full-field investigations are scheduled for completion in twenty-five to thirty-five days, but may take substantially longer if there are delays in the receipt of records and reports from other agencies, if the need arises for follow-up inquiries after the first level of interviews and review, or for other reasons which may be difficult to anticipate or predict. The FBI, however, routinely sends the White House partial results of the investigation while awaiting completion of the record.

Once completed, the results of the full-field investigation are sent to the Office of the Counsel to the President for evaluation. Routine and favorable information is summarized by the FBI, but the complete results of interviews of individuals who provide derogatory information are included so that the White House can make its own assessment. The counsel usually examines the file and reports the general results to the personnel office. Only if there is reason for particular concern does the president or his top aides examine the contents of the file.

The records of the full-field investigation are protected by the Privacy Act and are generally exempt from release under the Freedom of Information Act. The results are provided only to the White House. With the president's authorization, the record may also be shared with specific senators and staff members on the committee responsible for confirmation of the appointment. In general, access to the records is tightly held, and the FBI will only release results upon orders from the president or the attorney general. Leaks have sometimes occurred, however, on both ends of Pennsylvania Avenue.

PERSONAL BACKGROUND REVIEW

A third clearance is a thorough examination of the potential nominee's personal background and financial situation, supervised by the Office of the Counsel to the President. This begins with the completion by the nominee of a personal data statement, a lengthy list of questions on such matters as the previous involvement of the candidate in criminal or civil litigation, the candidate's business associations, controversial public statements made by the candidate, and any other information which, if made public, might prove harmful or embarrassing to the nominee or the president. Among the questions included by recent administrations have been these:

- Have you ever been publicly identified, in person or by organizational membership, with a particularly controversial national or local issue?

- Have you ever submitted oral or written views to any government authority (executive or legislative) or the news media on any particularly controversial issue other than in an official governmental capacity?

- Have you ever written any particularly controversial books or articles?

- Have you ever had any association with any person or group or business venture which could be used, even unfairly, to impugn or attack your appointment?

All of this information is for internal White House use only; none
of it is made public. Once this statement has been completed, it is submitted to the counsel's office where it is subject to careful review. The
candidate may well be asked to clarify any information that seems
incomplete or potentially troublesome.

Recent administrations have also engaged in an elaborate process
of reference checking called "vetting." While the vetting process has
come to light more fully during the Clinton transition than ever
before, it is not a recent invention. Both Kennedy and Johnson
recruiters used "contact networks" to help them find and evaluate
potential nominees. The first of these was set up and funded by the
Brookings Institution for President Kennedy. Some degree of vetting
has occurred in all subsequent administrations.

<h3 style="text-align:center">CONFLICT OF INTEREST</h3>

The Ethics in Government Act of 1978 added a fat new layer to
the appointment process. Elaborate routines now exist for prepara-
tion and review of the financial disclosure reports filed by candidates
for presidential appointments. Several organizations participate in
this review and pass judgment on compliance with the ethics laws.
The Office of Government Ethics (OGE) was established by the Ethics
in Government Act of 1978 and charged with responsibility for overall direction of executive branch conflict of interest policies. Attorneys
at OGE assist presidential appointees and other executive branch
officials in interpreting and complying with the ethics laws.

The Counsel to the President heads a staff of attorneys. In a
sense, the counsel's office is the president's law firm, and in that role
one of its responsibilities is to ensure that all of the president's
appointees comply with the conflict of interest laws. It works closely
with OGE and agency ethics officers to accomplish that. Typically, a
draft of the financial disclosure form (SF 278) is prepared and discussions occur between the nominee and the counsel's staff about
potential conflict-of-interest problems and ways to resolve them. This
provides an opportunity for the nominee to anticipate potential conflicts of interest and to deal with them before the disclosure form is
made public.

Once the disclosure forms have been completed, the report is
sent to the designated agency ethics officer (DAEO) in the agency in
which the nominee will serve. The DAEO is usually a member of the
agency's legal staff who is designated by the head of the agency to

coordinate and manage its ethics program. The DAEO reviews the forms to ensure that the nominee's financial interests and activities comply with the conflict-of-interest laws and regulations that apply to all government employees and with any other statute or regulation applicable only to employees of that agency.

If the DAEO believes that the financial disclosure form reveals a potential conflict of interest, he or she will notify the nominee of that opinion and afford the nominee an opportunity for personal consultation. After discussing these matters with the nominee, the DAEO will notify the nominee in writing of the remedial actions that must be taken to achieve compliance with the applicable conflict-of-interest laws and regulations. This written notification will also indicate a date by which such remedial action must be undertaken.

Once the DAEO has concluded that there is no conflict of interest under applicable laws and regulations, he or she forwards the financial disclosure form to the Office of Government Ethics, attaching a copy of the official job description of the position to be filled by the nominee. In addition, the DAEO personally certifies the financial disclosure report and dates that certification. Along with the report, the DAEO sends the director of the OGE an opinion letter certifying that there is no conflict of interest, discussing any problems encountered in reaching the conclusions on which the certification is based, and describing the resolution of those problems. In this opinion letter, the DAEO will also discuss any specific agreement, commitment, recusal, or other undertaking by the nominee to resolve a potential conflict of interest.

The director of the OGE reviews the material received from the agency and, if satisfied that there is no unresolved conflict of interest, signs and dates the financial disclosure report. If the appointment requires Senate confirmation, the report is then forwarded to the Senate committee with jurisdiction over the nomination. It is accompanied by a letter from the director of the OGE expressing the director's opinion that, on the basis of the information provided in the financial disclosure report, the nominee is in compliance with the applicable conflict-of-interest laws and regulations.

The DAEOs and the OGE attorneys function more as problem solvers than prosecutors. They work with nominees to identify potential conflicts of interest and to seek ways to "cure" them. The OGE attempts, in the words of J. Jackson Walter, its first director, to serve as "a law firm and consulting firm for the agencies and departments" on conflict-of-interest issues.[3] Negotiation, as Walter noted, is often the key ingredient in this clearance process:

> There is a considerable amount of business back and forth between the Counsel's office and the OGE staff attempting to identify and resolve questions before the Counsel's office says OK. OGE's approach was that surprise was a lousy regulatory procedure and that notoriety was not supposed to be the outcome of this process. We very much approached all of the cases that I remember with the notion that we were problem solvers. If you have a problem, let's try to identify it with some real specificity and then figure out how to cure it.[4]

The only known study of the impact of conflict-of-interest requirements on new presidential appointees was conducted by the National Academy of Public Administration in the mid-1980s. Its findings are based on a survey of appointees who actually served and thus does not include the experiences of those not nominated or confirmed because of conflict-of-interest problems. The findings, displayed in Table 2.1, indicate the actions taken to comply with conflict-of-interest laws by appointees serving between mid-1979 and late 1984.

TABLE 2.1
COMPLIANCE ACTIONS REQUIRED OF PRESIDENTIAL APPOINTEES SERVING JUNE 1979–DECEMBER 1984

COMPLIANCE ACTION	PERCENTAGE OF APPOINTEES
No action required	32.8
Created blind trust	11.6
Created diversified trust	1.5
Sold stock or other assets	32.3
Resigned positions in corporations or other organizations	40.9
Executed recusal statement	16.7

Note: Total exceeds 100 percent because some appointees were required to take more than one compliance action.

Source: National Academy of Public Administration, Appointee Survey Data Base, 1985.

SENATE CONFIRMATION

In the vast majority of cases, confirmation occurs routinely after the Senate has reviewed the credentials of nominees submitted by the president. Despite the heavy press attention paid to some confirmation controversies—in recent years, for example, to those of Edwin Meese, Robert Bork, John Tower, Clarence Thomas, Zoë Baird, and Lani Guinier—most confirmations occur without controversy and with little public notice. While confirmation proceedings vary in many ways, their principal elements are described here.

The formalities of the confirmation process are simple and routine. Presidents transmit their nominations by message to the Senate. Upon arrival there, the message is read on the Senate floor, received by the parliamentarian, and assigned a consecutive number by the executive clerk. Nominations are then referred to an individual committee (or, in a few cases, to several committees) for review.

The procedures for committee review are established by individual committees and vary widely. The individual Senate committees conduct their own reviews of a nominee's finances and potential conflicts of interest—reviews governed by committee rules and traditions rather than statutes and regulations. Committees have their own questionnaires and forms for nominees to complete, and these are not consistent from one committee to the next. The procedures of the Armed Services Committee, for example, are markedly different from those of the Judiciary Committee. Committee chairs, staff, and sometimes individual members may also make written interrogatories of nominees. Nominees often complain that the requirements and forms imposed on them by Senate committees are sufficiently different from those employed by the White House and the OGE that a significant additional burden of information gathering and reporting is added to the appointment process when a nomination goes to the Senate.

It is a common view among veteran committee staff members that the Senate cannot rely solely on FBI investigations. It was noted at the time of the Clarence Thomas nomination, for example, that Anita Hill's name never surfaced in any of the full-field investigations the FBI conducted for the several federal nominations Clarence Thomas had previously received. Similarly, in 1987, the marijuana use that sunk the nomination of Douglas Ginsburg to the Supreme Court was turned up by a reporter and missed completely by the FBI. Other such gaps and oversights have left a legacy of Senate skepticism about FBI background investigations.[5]

Confirmation hearings are conducted by Senate committees. Most hearings are brief, perfunctory, and friendly—like welcoming a new member to a club. Others operate like job interviews where individual senators use the hearing to inform the nominee of their pet interests and concerns, of issues worrying their constituents, or of pitfalls into which previous appointees have fallen. Senators routinely seek to extract promises from nominees during these hearings as a way to guide or constrain future administrative action. As I have written elsewhere,

> ... the Senate uses its confirmation power as part of an arsenal of weapons for influencing the shape and direction of public policy. . . . It can, of course, reject a nominee and indicate to the president that it did so because it found his policy views unacceptable. But it does not often do that. More commonly, the Senate uses its power of rejection as a threat. It may withhold action on a nomination until the nominee or the White House agrees to pursue certain courses of action about which the members of the Senate committee feel strongly. It may require the nominee, as a condition of his confirmation, to make policy-related promises to the committee during the confirmation hearing. Or it may use its power to delay or reject a nominee as a bargaining chip to force the administration into some policy action unrelated to the nomination in question. The confirmation power is thus a versatile tool for the Senate in its efforts to enlarge its influence on public policy decisions.[6]

The vigor and rigor of Senate confirmation proceedings took a dramatic turn in the mid-1970s. In 1977, remarkable as it now seems, Common Cause published a study of the confirmation process, *The Senate Rubberstamp Machine*, in which it criticized the Senate's lack of diligence in reviewing presidential appointments. But political hostility between president and Congress was brewing at this time, spurred in large part by the persistence of divided government and the excesses of the Nixon administration. The Senate Commerce Committee, with Warren Magnuson in the chair and Michael Pertschuk as staff director, took the lead in developing new procedures for, and increasing the intensity of, confirmation investigations and hearings. Other committees quickly followed suit, and by the early 1980s, even a Republican-controlled Senate was aggressively reviewing and occasionally rejecting Ronald Reagan's nominations.

Table 2.2 indicates the full scope of Senate confirmation authority. The Senate's real focus is much narrower, however, concentrating on the several hundred appointments with the greatest impact on public policy. These generally now receive the careful scrutiny of

TABLE 2.2
CONFIRMATION JURISDICTION AND ACTIONS OF THE U.S. SENATE, 1929–1992

Cong.	Years	Received	SENATE ACTION Confirmed	Withdrawn	Rejected*	Unconfirmed
72d	1931–33	12,716	10,909	19	1	1,787
73d	1933–34	9,094	9,027	17	3	47
74th	1935–36	22,487	22,286	51	15	135
75th	1937–38	15,330	15,193	20	27	90
76th	1939–41	29,072	28,939	16	21	96
77th	1941–42	24,344	24,137	33	5	169
78th	1943–44	21,775	21,371	31	6	367
79th	1945–46	37,022	36,550	17	3	452
80th	1947–48	66,641	54,796	153	0	11,692
81st	1949–51	87,266	86,562	45	6	653
82d	1951–52	46,920	46,504	45	2	369
83rd	1953–54	69,458	68,563	43	0	852
84th	1955–56	84,173	82,694	38	3	1,438
85th	1957–58	104,193	103,311	54	0	828
86th	1959–60	91,476	89,900	30	1	1,545
87th	1961–62	102,849	100 741	1,279	0	829
88th	1963–64	122,190	120 201	36	0	1,953
89th	1965–66	123,019	120 865	173	0	1,981
90th	1967–68	120,231	118 231	34	0	1,966
91st	1969–71	134,464	133 797	487	2	178
92d	1971–72	117,053	114 909	11	0	2,133
93d	1973–74	134,384	131 254	15	0	3,069
94th	1975–76	132,151	131 378	6	0	3,801
95th	1977–78	137,504	124 730	66	0	12,713
96th	1979–80	154,797	154 665	18	0	1,458
97th	1981–82	186,264	184 844	55	7	1,346
98th	1983–84	97,893	97,262	4	0	610
99th	1985–86	99,614	95,811	16	0	3,787
100th	1987–88	89,193	88,721	23	1	5,922
101st	1989–90	93,368	88,078	48	1	7,951
102d	1991–92	76,446	75,349	24	0	756
103d	1993–94	77,384	76,122	1,080	0	2,741

* Includes only those nominations rejected outright by Senate vote, not those withdrawn or terminated earlier in the process.

Source: Adapted from Harold W. Stanley and Richard G. Niemi, *Vital Statistics on American Politics,* 4th and 5th eds. (Washington, D.C.: Congressional Quarterly Press, 1994 and 1995).

Senate committee staffs and sometimes individual senator's staffs as well. Formal hearings are held on most of them. Senators and committees now do a good deal of vetting on their own.

In a small minority of confirmation hearings, attention focuses on some aspect of the nominee's experience or views that troubles some senators. These are often the confirmation hearings that attract press attention. Just in the first year of the Clinton administration, for example, Senate committees focused intense attention on Zoë Baird's household employment practices, Lani Guinier's writing on apportionment and minority voting, Morton Halperin's views on use of military force and covert operations abroad, and Roberta Achtenberg's opposition to funding for the Boy Scouts of San Francisco. The confirmation hearings of that small group of nominees received more public attention than those of hundreds of other Clinton appointees who were confirmed routinely. This imbalance in coverage contributes to a growing public perception—and a perception among potential nominees—that confirmation hearings are typically demeaning and brutal assaults on the reputations of presidential appointees.

One important consequence of the increased attention that Senate committees now pay to their confirmation duties is that the confirmation process takes longer to unfold than ever before. Table 2.3 indicates how the process lengthened over the years from 1964 through 1984.

TABLE 2.3
NUMBER OF WEEKS FROM RECEIPT OF NOMINATION TO CONFIRMATION BY THE SENATE, 1964–1984

ADMINISTRATION	MEAN	MEDIAN
Johnson	6.8	4.0
Nixon	8.5	7.0
Ford	11.0	8.0
Carter	11.8	10.0
Reagan (through 1984)	14.6	14.0

Source: Adapted from Christopher J. Deering, "Damned If You Do and Damned If You Don't: The Senate's Role in the Appointments Process," in G. Calvin Mackenzie, ed., *The In and Outers* (Baltimore, Maryland: Johns Hopkins University Press, 1987), p. 112. Data for this table were drawn from the National Academy of Public Administration Appointee Survey Data Base and are derived from individual PAS appointees' reports of the time required for their confirmations.

A longer confirmation process is frustrating for both presidents and nominees. Presidents and department and agency heads wait for months for nominees to get through the Senate before they can fully engage their new jobs. While many nominees do spend time in the offices to which they've been nominated while their confirmations are under consideration, they are tightly constrained in their ability to participate in decisionmaking because they lack formal authority and because most are reluctant to state views for which they might have to answer later at confirmation hearings.

These delays are frustrating to nominees not only for this reason, but for financial reasons as well. Typically, nominees will begin to separate from their previous employment as soon as they've been selected by the president for an administration appointment. But then it may well be months before they get their first paycheck and come under benefit coverage of the federal government. The length and uncertainty of the confirmation process makes this a harrowing time for many nominees.

Committees are the most important decision units in the confirmation process. Rare indeed is the nomination that gets to the floor without committee approval. Once they've voted on nominations, committees report them favorably or unfavorably to the full Senate. These reports are filed with the legislative clerk and then assigned an executive calendar number by the executive clerk. In general, nominations are considered by the full Senate on the first day they appear on the executive calendar. Nearly all are approved by the Senate, usually with little debate and by unanimous consent. On appointment confirmations, extensive floor debate and roll call votes are rarities. But, again, the rarities get the bulk of the press coverage.

3

THE CLINTON TRANSITION

The Clinton transition illustrates in full color the complexities of the contemporary presidential appointment process. No one familiar with the realities of the process thought it would be easy to staff the Clinton administration. It was, in fact, more difficult than even the pessimists anticipated.

Part of the story was that President Clinton encountered all of the continuing and normal problems of staffing a presidential administration. The number of PAS (presidential appointment requiring Senate confirmation) positions continues to grow. Because of the complex responsibilities that fall on the holders of those positions, recruiters must find appointees with special expertise and experience. The principal components of the appointment process—ethics and personal background checks, FBI investigations, and Senate confirmation—are elaborate and time-consuming. The low esteem of public service, the lack of funds for bold new programs, and persistent low government salaries deter many talented people from accepting or even considering a presidential appointment. Aggressive senators and jugular-seeking reporters and columnists terrify others.

All of the recent presidents have had to endure these difficulties in staffing their administrations. The process has taken more time and yielded much more frustration than any of them anticipated. Jimmy Carter said, "I have learned in my first two and a half weeks why Abraham Lincoln and some of the older presidents went home when they first got to the White House. The handling of personnel appointments, trying to get the right person in the right position at the right time, is a very difficult question." Ronald Reagan, when asked at a press conference if there was anything he was not pleased with in his first two months in office, said: "Yes, the slowness in filling appointments . . . part of our delay has been the new rules and regulations that have been passed and imposed that makes clearance of appointees take longer than it formerly did."

But for Bill Clinton were a few special problems as well—some inevitable, some self-induced. After Republican control of the White House for the past twelve years and twenty of the previous twenty-four years, Clinton found no government-in-waiting. Because Democrats with successful and significant federal experience were so scarce, Clinton had to search harder and wider for his appointees than is the norm. This is reflected in the composition of his first Cabinet. Its fourteen members included only four who had held previous office in the executive branch, only two of them at the assistant secretary level or above.

Clinton was further handicapped by his own limited experience in Washington. Though he was widely regarded as remarkably well-connected, especially among the political and intellectual leaders of his generation, he was a stranger to most members of Congress and to much of the Washington power structure. The desire to build an administration that could succeed politically and legislatively took considerable time because Clinton's own instincts required some honing.

Early in the transition, Clinton exacerbated the difficulties he faced by promising to select an "administration that looked like America." His recruiters employed what some called the "EGG standard," looking for appointees of diverse ethnicity, gender, and geography. Accounts at the end of his first year in office indicated that Clinton had succeeded notably in accomplishing this. His appointees at that point included larger percentages of females, African-Americans, and Hispanics than any previous administration.[1] But the commitment to diversity slowed the staffing process. Female and minority appointees are harder to find than white males; they do not inhabit the on-deck circles from which potential presidential appointees have traditionally come.

The Clinton process seems unique not for its novelty but its intensity. Vetting of Clinton nominees during the early months of the transition was conducted largely outside the White House by volunteer teams of more than one hundred people, many of them lawyers. They worked the phones aggressively to check and cross-check references on candidates for appointment, to verify items in their resumes, and to poke relentlessly into closets where skeletons might lurk. The team that vetted the highly sensitive nomination of Janet Reno, for example, made more than two hundred such calls. Among the issues normally probed by the Clinton vetters were emotional problems, alcohol or drug abuse, arrests or business investigations, and past affiliations—anything, broadly defined, that might undermine a nomination or embarrass the president.[2]

The staffing of the Clinton administration was slowed in another way as well. From the start, personnel selection was burdened by inconsistent and unclear divisions of labor and responsibility. Several younger Clinton aides were given pieces of the personnel planning process before the election. After Clinton won, he designated former governor Richard Riley of South Carolina to take charge of staffing the administration. Riley had no special experience in this and no personal familiarity with the positions he was filling or the unique politics of each. In any case, he quickly emerged as Clinton's nominee to be secretary of education, and his attention diverted away from personnel matters. Riley was succeeded as personnel chief by Bruce Lindsey, a longtime Clinton aide and confidant. But Lindsey continued to carry other responsibilities and often traveled with the president.

All of this meant that the transition personnel operation lacked a strong center. Cabinet secretaries and agency heads went their own way in seeking appointees for top-level positions in their organizations. When they submitted these for approval at the White House, however, their lists were often bounced back because they failed to meet the EGG standard or because the personnel office or the president had other candidates in mind. Time was inevitably lost in these exchanges between the White House and the departments and agencies. When Agriculture Secretary Mike Espy sent over his list of sub-cabinet candidates, for example, the White House sent it back because it included too many men. Similarly, Henry Cisneros's choices for HUD were thought by the White House to include too many New Yorkers.

The construction of the Clinton administration was also influenced by the need to coordinate several intersecting power centers. Hillary Rodham Clinton played a significant role; so, too, did Vice President Al Gore. Warren Christopher had significant influence in the immediate post-election period. The president himself was more actively involved in selection decisions than any president since Lyndon Johnson. The need to navigate and broker these multiple power centers and to endure a presidential decisionmaking style that comes slowly to closure elongated the staffing process.

It is important to note as well that Clinton encountered more and higher appointment hurdles than any of his predecessors. Appointment choices, like all policy choices, are now deeply complicated by Washington's constantly intensifying interest group politics. The routine is now familiar: the president announces a nomination and the sides are quickly drawn. The groups that favor the nominee announce their support; the groups that dislike the nomination announce their opposition. Reporters soon begin sticking microphones in the faces of senators asking how they'll vote on the nomination. Investigative reporters start to dig. The battle is joined; the lobbying begins. In the absence of political bosses or effective political parties, no one seems able to constrain or referee these disagreements. So they are fought out, often viciously, in public. The process is slowed, and nominees often incur bruises and scars to their reputations.

Aggravating these tendencies are new technologies that have quickly become weapons in appointment combat. Nexis-Lexis makes it possible for interested participants to search out everything a nominee has ever written—and take it out of context and blow it out of proportion. Strobe Talbott's elevation to deputy secretary of state, for example, was slowed in the confirmation process by the discovery of old *Time* magazine columns in which he had suggested the need for the United States to rethink its strong support for Israel. Videotape provides a similar archive of past statements that may come back to haunt a nominee. History evaporates more slowly now than ever before.

Fax machines and electronic mail have affected the confirmation process by accelerating the impact of interest group influence. Groups can communicate more rapidly with their members about the "dangers" of a particular nomination; those members can communicate more quickly with their senators. The growing prominence of talk radio has also become a potent new force in the appointment process. Zoë Baird's nomination to be attorney general seemed likely to weather concerns about her household help problems until the talk shows stirred up firestorms of protest from which there was no escape.

The standards applied to President Clinton's nominees have been a constantly moving, constantly rising, target. As Clinton himself noted in an interview with Larry King after his first year in office:

> MR. KING: . . . Why in this year did we have so many appointment problems?

> THE PRESIDENT: First of all, I think most of it was because the rules changed on the household help issue. That had never been an issue before. And all of a sudden it was a big issue and the press was pillorying people that had the problem, and it was a problem. And so we had to get that worked out. I don't think it will ever happen again now because now there are fairly clear rules. . . .
> The second thing was that people's writings became an issue for jobs other than the Supreme Court. That is—Judge Bork's writings were an issue but that's because the Supreme Court got to read, interpret the Constitution and it was a lifetime job. The senators and others decided this year that they'd make that an issue for everybody for confirmation, which I think is a questionable standard, but it did.

> MR. KING: You're talking about Lani Guinier and—

> THE PRESIDENT: Yes. And one or two others that became an issue even though we got a couple through. So I think that there are—these standards are always being raised and heightened.

The change in standards for confirmation has been widely noted. As former Republican political aide Mitchell Daniels recently noted, there is "no issue too small, no sin too antique" for consideration by those who oppose a nomination. A president can never be sure that even a thoroughly "vetted" nominee will have an easy ride through the confirmation process because confirmation standards and the political circumstances that shape them are highly fluid. This adds more uncertainty to the appointment process and encourages more risk avoidance than ever before.

It also slows the process down, as Figure 3.1 indicates. The average length of time for selection and confirmation of PAS appointees has been growing over the past three decades. In the first year of the Clinton administration, it took longer than ever before.

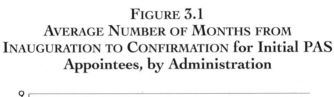

FIGURE 3.1
AVERAGE NUMBER OF MONTHS FROM
INAUGURATION TO CONFIRMATION for Initial PAS
Appointees, by Administration

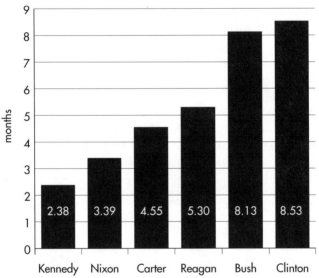

Source: Author calculation from data in *Congressional Quarterly Almanac* for 1961, 1969, 1977, 1981, and 1989. Data for Clinton administration is calculated by the author from reports prepared by Rogelio Garcia, Specialist in National Government, Government Division, Congressional Research Service. See *CRS Report to Congress: Presidential Appointments to Full-Time Positions in Executive Departments during the 103d Congress* (9–736 GOV, Revised December 29, 1993) and *CRS Report to Congress: Presidential Appointments to Full-Time Positions in Independent and Other Agencies, 103d Congress* (93–924 GOV, Revised December 30, 1993). Included in this calculation are PAS appointees in all of the cabinet departments and most of the large independent agencies. Regulatory commissions are not included, nor are inspectors general, ambassadors, U.S. attorneys, or U.S. marshals.

4

ISSUES AND SOLUTIONS

T he contemporary appointment process is burdened by many problems, but three stand out:

♦ *It takes too long for a new president to staff the senior positions in the administration.* As we've noted earlier, the length of time necessary to fill positions has grown steadily since the early 1960s. The average time now to fill a single position is around eight months. Our two most recent presidents were in office a year before half their senior positions were filled by a Senate-confirmed appointee of their choosing. A frustrated President Clinton said at the end of his first year: "I think, frankly, the process takes too long now. I talked to several Republicans and Democrats who have no particular axe to grind now who think maybe it's time to have a bipartisan look at this whole appointments process. It takes too long to get somebody confirmed. It's too bureaucratic. You have two and three levels of investigation. I think it's excessive." [1]

♦ *Nominees are exposed for too long to too much investigation and criticism.* The people who are selected as presidential appointees are among the most talented and successful American citizens. Yet the appointment process often treats them as potentially dangerous criminals. As David Gergen wrote in 1991, "If the nation is to restore a measure of civility and common purpose in meeting its domestic crises, it must find ways to end the relentless, ugly assaults upon the character of its public figures."[2]

◆ *Because the costs and risks of service are so high, it becomes increasingly difficult to recruit the highly qualified people necessary to manage the complex affairs of modern government.* Presidential recruiters report that many potential appointees don't even want to be considered for these jobs. Others permit themselves to be considered, then decline the jobs when offered. Increasingly, people now accept a nomination, then withdraw in exasperation before the appointment process is complete, as Bobby Inman and Stanley Tate did recently.[3] In our zeal to produce a government that is scandal-proof and error-proof, we have created a recruiting environment that is counterproductive to national needs.

What can be done to address these problems? Consensus on the nature and magnitude of the problems has not been matched by consensus on solutions, but some potential solutions are worth examining.

LIMITING THE NUMBER OF APPOINTED POSITIONS

Some have argued that the number of appointees has grown too large. A recent panel report of the National Academy of Public Administration took this position:

> This growth in the number of appointed positions places an increasing burden on the president's ability to locate and recruit qualified people to fill these posts and, where confirmation is required, on the Senate's ability to review appointees' credentials with care. The presidential appointments system is in jeopardy of overload. The capacity no longer exists—in the White House or in the Senate—to find and assess with care the qualifications of the large number of people now needed to fill all appointed positions.[4]

But efforts to convert some current PAS positions to PA or career senior executive jobs are often opposed by presidents or senators wishing to retain control over them. In 1988, for example, a modest congressional proposal (HR 2882) to cap the number of political appointees in grade GS–13 or above at one thousand—

roughly the current figure—was strongly opposed by the Reagan administration because it would "interfere with the responsiveness and efficiency of government management."[5] The number of PAS positions continues to grow because presidents oppose cutbacks in appointed personnel and because the Congress vigilantly defends its prerogative to participate through the confirmation process in the selection of these ever-expanding layers of federal managers.

REEXAMINE THE ETHICS RULES AND THEIR IMPLEMENTATION

Many voices have decried the increasing number and severity of federal ethics requirements. Critics argue that we demand too much information of too many senior executives reported in categories that are too demanding.[6] One senior Reagan appointee called it "a process twisted by knaves to make a trap for fools."[7] Some observers of the changes of the past decade and a half note that all these new ethics rules have not bought us much real improvement in the integrity of public officials, but have cost us a number of talented appointees who couldn't or wouldn't serve under rules that they believed far too draconian.[8]

There has, however, been little sustained effort to simplify or reduce ethical standards. Indeed, all of the momentum has been to broaden and tighten them. Both presidents Bush and Clinton raised the ante for their own appointees, requiring them to abide by more rigorous conflict-of-interest standards than their predecessors. Ethics is like motherhood; no one wants to oppose it. And even if the evidence suggests that tightening the standards may punish recruiting capabilities more than it improves integrity, the safe vote is always the one that seems to be for more ethics, not less. Thus there is no effective constituency in government for less rigid and restrictive conflict-of-interest rules.

RATIONALIZE NOMINEE BACKGROUND INVESTIGATIONS

The length of the appointment process is not the result of any single decision or any articulated desire. The process is composed of several parts, separately operated, designed to serve the different purposes of different institutions. Presidents, beginning in the early 1960s, sought to take control of the selection of nominees by creating an effective recruitment capability in the White House. As with most things bureaucratic, the Presidential Personnel Office grew in size and sophistication over the years. With that growth came an elongation of the time required to select nominees for executive branch positions. More recently, in the face of some political embarrassments, a more extensive vetting process has been added to presidential selection. Perhaps this has reduced the likelihood of embarrassing nominations—though the evidence on that is far from compelling—but it has certainly lengthened the selection process.

The FBI full-field investigation began in the Eisenhower administration. Almost every president since has complained about the length of these investigations. The FBI operates on its own timetable, however. Its principal objective is not to hurry but rather not to goof. There is nothing more exasperating to the leadership of the FBI than to submit an investigation report that fails to mention some criticism that is later uncovered in a confirmation hearing. Every time that happens, in fact, the FBI muscles up its own investigatory routines to prevent future recurrences.

CONTROL THE CONFIRMATION PROCESS

When the Senate began in the 1970s to take its confirmation responsibilities much more seriously than it ever had before, most scholars and editorial writers applauded. This was the immediate aftermath of Watergate, and any sign of congressional initiative seemed welcome. Over the years, however, the confirmation process has become something of a monster. Even the Senate can no longer fully control it. Confirmation of a single appointee can drag on for months, sometimes for a half year or more. Committees often duplicate investigations and reporting requirements that have already been completed elsewhere. Senators may use an appointment as a hostage in some unrelated political bargaining in which they're engaged. And confirmation hearings, with increasing frequency, have become ugly spectacles of contemporary American politics. No meaningful rules of evidence apply; senators may question nominees on whatever they wish. The show often has less to do with the nominee's qualifications or the issues he or she will be confronting than with the constituents or interest groups that senators hope to impress.

Frequent and public confirmation proceedings are a relatively recent phenomenon. Until 1929, nearly all confirmation debates were held in executive (that is, secret) session by the Senate. The first public confirmation hearing occurred on the Supreme Court nomination of Louis Brandeis in 1916, but nominees themselves rarely appeared to testify in any confirmation hearing before World War II. Felix Frankfurter, for example, initially turned down the invitation of the Senate Judiciary Committee to testify on his own appointment to the Supreme Court, maintaining that he did not want to skip the law classes he taught at Harvard. The standing rules of the Senate were not modified to require public confirmation hearings until 1975. No confirmation hearings were televised until 1969 when the Senate considered Walter Hickel's nomination as secretary of the interior. Some have suggested the desirability of reducing the number of public confirmation hearings. President George Bush, for example, proposed that Senate committees go into executive session to review messy personal matters. "I think sometimes when you get to subjects that are that sensitive, it is well to delegate to your elected officials," Bush said.[9]

Holding confirmation hearings in executive session, a practice that was once quite normal on Capitol Hill for business of all kinds, has fallen into disuse and disrepute of late. An option short of closing an entire hearing is to close those portions of the hearing that deal with questions of character or personal life or where criticisms of a nominee are based on testimony of others. Yet another possibility is to allow senators to submit written questions to a nominee and to decide after the answers have been submitted whether to hold a public hearing at all; such a decision might require the vote of a third (or some other percentage) of the members of the committee. But there has not been much Senate interest in suggestions like these—perhaps not surprisingly. In fact, the Senate Task Force on the Confirmation Process argued in 1991 that: "The confirmation hearing is the only point in the appointment process of federal officials that offers the public an opportunity to evaluate the qualifications of a nominee. The Senate has taken this obligation seriously and believes that the public hearing process is vital to the Senate's constitutional role of 'advice and consent.'"[10]

PLAYING FAIR

What is especially clear to many long-term observers is that the appointment process has become a meat grinder. Former Surgeon General Jocelyn Elders framed the problem poignantly in a recent interview: "I felt it was more a mechanism to try to destroy me than anything else. I came to Washington, D.C., like prime steak and after being here a while, I feel like poor grade hamburger."[11]

The cost of this is very high. Committed, talented American leaders suffer unfair assaults and lingering damage to their reputations. Many others decline appointments—or decline even to be considered for appointments—because they have no stomach and no need for the culture of mistrust that now engulfs Washington.

Thus we confront a peculiar irony: the decades-old effort to improve the process of selecting and confirming presidential appointees has produced an outcome directly opposite its intentions. It repels the appointees it ought to attract. It shortens the tenure in office it ought to sustain. It corrodes the reputations it ought to embellish. More and more, as its victims fall, the presidential appointment process becomes an impediment to the president, a repellent to public servants, and a deterrent to good government. The late Yale president, A. Bartlett Giamatti, once wrote, "If a society assumes its politicians are venal, stupid or self-serving, it will attract to its public life as an on-going self-fulfilling prophecy the greedy, the knavish and the dim."[12]

It is a danger we must all take seriously as it looms ever larger before us.

A Sampler of Ethics Rules for Presidential Appointees

Public Disclosure of Personal Finances

At the time of appointment and annually thereafter, every presidential appointee must make full disclosure of the source and categories of value of all income, property investments and assets, compensation, positions held, and liabilities. Disclosure must also be made for the appointee's spouse and dependent children.

Official Conduct in Office

Supplementation of Salary

Basic Rule: No executive branch official may have his or her salary supplemented by nongovernment sources. Supplementation of salary is any cash, property, or other gift of value intended to increase the compensation of federal employees, whether or not special favor is expected in return.

Self-dealing

Basic Rule: No executive branch employee may engage in any government activity or decision in which he or she has a direct financial interest.

Among the potential instruments for avoiding conflicts of interest are:

◆   Divestiture

◆   Recusal/Disqualification

◆   Qualified blind trust

◆   Qualified diversified trust

◆   Waivers

ACCEPTANCE OF GIFTS, GRATUITIES, ENTERTAINMENT, AND TRAVEL

Basic Rule: Often, as part of official duties, federal executives meet with representatives of organizations that are regulated by or seek to do business with their agency. Federal law strictly limits the ability of federal employees to accept items of value from such private sources.

OUTSIDE INCOME AND ACTIVITIES

Basic Rule: Current regulations strictly limit the receipt of earned income from nongovernment sources by executive branch employees. Presidential appointees may accept no outside earned income, including honoraria.

MISUSE OF GOVERNMENT PROPERTY

Basic Rule: Government employees may not use government property for private purposes or "for other than officially approved activities."

MISUSE OF GOVERNMENT INFORMATION

Basic Rule: Information available to government officials should not be used for any private purpose or advantage.

POST-EMPLOYMENT RESTRICTIONS

NEGOTIATING FOR FUTURE EMPLOYMENT

Basic Rule: Government employees should consider a potential future employer, with whom negotiations for employment are underway or anticipated, as a source of conflict of interest and withdraw from any government activity or decisions involving that potential future employer.

Restrictions on Post-employment Representation and Service

Basic Rule: Former government employees are strictly limited in representing private parties before their former agencies and in matters in which the former employee participated personally and substantially while in government.

There are several fundamental restrictions on post-employment activities:

1. A lifetime ban against acting as a representative on "particular matters" in which an individual "personally and substantially" participated as a government employee.

2. A two-year ban on representing anyone on matters that were within the former employee's official responsibilities during the last year of service.

3. A two-year ban on certain former "senior employees," prohibiting their representation "by personal presence" in particular matters in which they participated personally.

4. A one-year ban on communications by former senior officials made with intent to influence their former agencies in any particular matter pending before that agency.

5. A one-year ban on former cabinet secretaries and senior White House officials lobbying any other senior executive branch official on any subject.

6. A one-year ban on all former presidential appointees from lobbying for a foreign government.

"Appearance" of Impropriety or Conflict of Interest

Basic Rule: Government employees shall endeavor to avoid any actions, such as those listed below, which create the appearance that they are violating the law or ethical standards. Whether particular circumstances create an appearance that the law or these standards have been violated shall be determined from the perspective of a reasonable person with knowledge of the relevant facts.

- Using public office for private gain

- Giving preferential treatment to any person

- Impeding government efficiency or economy

- Losing complete independence or impartiality

- Making a government decision outside of official channels

- Affecting adversely the confidence of the public in the integrity of the government

NOTES

1

1. U.S. Department of Commerce, Bureau of the Census, *Historical Statistics of the United States, Colonial Times to 1970* (Washington, D.C.: Government Printing Office, 1975), pp. 1100, 1105.

2. Panel on Presidentially Appointed Scientists and Engineers, National Academy of Sciences, *Science and Technology Leadership in American Government: Ensuring the Best Presidential Appointments* (Washington, D.C.: National Academy Press, 1992), p. 1.

3. Dan H. Fenn, Jr., "Dilemmas for the Regulator," *California Management Review* (Spring 1974): 88.

4. *Recruiting Presidential Appointees: A Conference of Former Presidential Personnel Assistants* (Washington, D.C.: National Academy of Public Administration, 1984), p. 5.

5. Dan H. Fenn, Jr., interview with the author, Waltham, Massachusetts, March 26, 1976.

6. U.S. Senate, Committee on Government Operations, *The Regulatory Appointments Process* (Washington, D.C.: Government Printing Office, 1977), p. 123.

7. Frederic V. Malek, *Washington's Hidden Tragedy* (New York: The Free Press, 1978), p. 63.

8. Quoted in Dom Bonafede, "Nixon Personnel Staff Works to Restructure Federal Policies," *National Journal* (November 12, 1971), p. 2446.

2

1. E. Pendleton James, interview with the author, Washington, D.C., July 13, 1981.

2. *Recruiting Presidential Appointees: A Conference of Former Presidential Personnel Assistants* (Washington, D.C.: National Academy of Public Administration, 1984), p. 4.

3. U.S. Senate, Committee on Governmental Affairs, Subcommittee on Oversight of Government Management, *Hearing on Reauthorization of the Office of Government Ethics*, February 24, 1983, p. 51.

4. J. Jackson Walter, interview with the author, Washington, D.C., November 14, 1984.

5. Joan Biskupic, "FBI Background Investigations Draw Intensified Scrutiny," *Congressional Quarterly Weekly Report*, April 1, 1989, pp. 699–701.

6. G. Calvin Mackenzie, *The Politics of Presidential Appointments* (New York: Free Press, 1981), p. 134.

3

1. See Martha Farnsworth Riche, "The Bean Count Is In!" *Washington Post*, January 23, 1994, p. C2.

2. Burt Soloman, "The True Secrets of Clintonite . . . Linger Behind The 'Vetting' Veil," *National Journal*, March 13, 1993, p. 644.

4

1. "Remarks by the President During Larry King Live," White House Press Office Transcript, January 20, 1994.

2. David Gergen, "How to Improve the Process," *U.S. News and World Report*, October 28, 1991, p. 39.

3. Inman was nominated to be secretary of defense; Tate was nominated to head the Resolution Trust Corporation. Tate withdrew after waiting four months for the Senate to confirm his appointment. He said at the time that the delay was the "most difficult and stressful involvement in his life" and left him feeling "disposable and dispensable." See John H. Cushman, Jr., "Nominee for Bailout Agency Bitterly Withdraws His Name," *New York Times*, December 1, 1993, p. A1.

4. *Leadership in Jeopardy: The Fraying of the Presidential Appointments System* (Washington, D.C.: National Academy of Public Administartion, 1985), p. 4.

5. Richard Cowan, "Panel OKs Bill Limiting Presidential Appointees," *Congressional Quarterly Weekly Report*, June 11, 1988, p. 1603.

6. See, for example, "Ethics Law Makes the Choice That Much Harder," *New York Times*, December 14, 1980.

7. Anonymous interview with Presidential Appointee Project staff, National Academy of Public Administration, 1985.

8. This argument is presented more fully in G. Calvin Mackenzie, "If You Want to Play, You've Got to Pay: Ethics Regulation and the Presidential Appointments System, 1964–1984" in Mackenzie, ed., *The In and Outers* (Baltimore, Maryland: Johns Hopkins University Press, 1987).

9. Quoted in Michael Wines, "Bush Says He Would Favor Closed Sessions," *New York Times*, October 18, 1991.

10. *Report of the Task Force on the Confirmation Process*, United States Senate, Washington, D.C., December 18, 1991, mimeo, p. 8.

11. Claudia Dreifus, "Jocelyn Elders," *New York Times Magazine*, January 30, 1994, p. 18.

12. A. Bartlett Giamatti, *The University and the Public Interest* (New York: Atheneum, 1981), p. 168.

THE CONFIRMATION WARS:
HOW POLITICIANS, INTEREST GROUPS, AND THE PRESS SHAPE THE PRESIDENTIAL APPOINTMENT PROCESS

ROBERT SHOGAN

1

INTRODUCTION

When President Clinton nominated Judge Stephen Breyer for the Supreme Court last spring, Clinton was counting on avoiding controversy in the Senate. The president had earlier appeared to have all but made up his mind to select Secretary of the Interior Bruce Babbitt for the vacancy created by the retirement of Justice Harry Blackmun.[1] But when opposition to Babbitt developed on Capitol Hill, and from right-wing interest groups, Breyer loomed as by far the safer choice. His support in the Senate Judiciary Committee ranged from Democratic Senator Edward M. Kennedy of Massachusetts on the left to the ranking Republican, Orrin Hatch of Utah, on the right.[2] Yet when Breyer's confirmation hearings got under way, the widely respected jurist had to fend off conflict of interest allegations from senators on both sides of the aisle, concerning his investment in a Lloyds of London insurance syndicate, before the way could be cleared for his Senate confirmation.[3]

The last-minute assault on Clinton's supposedly noncontroversial nominee and the circumstances surrounding his selection were the latest demonstration that, for high profile presidential appointments, the once easy path to confirmation has been transformed into a potential minefield. Years ago the assumption was that, within reasonable bounds, the president could appoint whomever he wanted to appoint. But, says Boston University political scientist Mark Silverstein, a specialist in the new politics of the appointment process: "Now the rule seems to be: 'Who can we get through without a fight?'"[4]

This paper will examine the interconnected forces that have contributed to this escalation of acrimony, with particular reference to the role of interest groups and the press. My brief is to concentrate on the struggle over what I have referred to as "high profile" positions—the Supreme Court, the cabinet, and those subcabinet nominations made by President Clinton and his six most recent predecessors that for one reason or another became the center of public controversy. Of course, many appointments down the executive ladder also attract opposition. But it is the battles over the higher-level jobs that best demonstrate the interplay of forces with which this paper is concerned. These marquee confrontations draw the interest of the press and engage the attention of the public, and their symbolic and practical significance produce a great expenditure of resources from contending interest groups.

This background paper will attempt to make two principal contributions to the work of the Task Force: First, it will analyze the most notable battles over nominations of the recent and not-so-recent past to bring historical perspective to the current tensions. Second, it will provide the admittedly self-interested but nonetheless informative views of a cross section of journalists and interest group leaders to add the perspective of those directly involved in the process.

In carrying out this study, I have drawn on my experience of more than twenty-five years as a Washington correspondent—in terms of the nominating process, a period encompassed at the start by Lyndon Johnson's abortive nomination of Abe Fortas to be chief justice and currently by Clinton's choice of Breyer. The conclusions are based largely on interviews conducted specifically for this paper with more than two dozen persons directly involved in the process: journalists in both the print and electronic media and interest group activists reaching across the ideological board—from Paul Weyrich of the Free Congress Foundation on the right to Ralph Neas of the Leadership Conference on Civil Rights on the left.

The principal conclusions supported by my case-by-case examination of the appointment process are as follows:

◆   A series of interrelated forces and developments over the past half century, notably the fragmentation of society and advances in communications technology, have eroded the strength of political parties and destabilized the political process, generating a volatility demonstrated most recently by the stunning transfer of power from Democrats to Republicans on Capitol Hill in the November 1994 elections. All this has created the potential for turning nearly every major presidential appointment into a battlefield. Among the factors that have been both cause and consequence of this trend are the rise of judicial activism, the extended period of divided government during the past three decades, and the decentralization of power on Capitol Hill.

◆   The interest groups that have proliferated across the spectrum, both as cause and effect of the erosion of parties, increasingly have become a force in the appointment process, second in importance only to the president. The interest groups cannot always decide who gets confirmed and who gets rejected, but they can determine who gets contested—and that is sufficient to give them plenty of weight with both the executive and legislative branches.

◆   The media have become a significant factor in contributing to the rise of contentiousness in the confirmation process. But the media do not drive the process. Rather, their role reflects the fundamental upheaval in the political system and the stratagems of the interest groups.

The complexity of the causes underlying the rise in contentiousness over nominations is clearly illustrated by the record of the Clinton presidency regarding high-level nominees. The controversies—which resulted at a time when both the White House, with its constitutionally mandated authority to nominate, and the Senate, with its responsibility to advise and consent, were both controlled by the Democratic party—make it clear that the diagnosis of divided government offered by many analysts to explain the bitter appointment battles during the twelve Reagan-Bush years is only part of the answer.

To be sure, most of the myriad of federal appointees still get by the Senate with little trouble, and often with little attention paid to their qualifications, or lack thereof. "Part of the irony about this contentiousness is that for most appointments, the Senate treats the appointment process as routine and doesn't pay much attention to it all," points out Common Cause president Fred Wertheimer.[5]

Indeed, to some minds, the Senate's handling of Breyer's confirmation was the latest example of the "routine treatment" syndrome.

Disturbed by Breyer's failure as an appeals court judge to recuse himself from major pollution disputes, even though he had a financial
stake in a Lloyds of London venture that insured against pollution
risks, the *New York Times* complained that "Senators of both parties are
rushing to a floor vote without fully investigating significant ethical
issues connected to the nominee's investments."[6]

But whatever the *Times* thought, it was clearly a welcome relief for
President Clinton when, a few days later, the judge was easily confirmed by the Senate by a vote of 87 to 8.[7] For in the previous months,
as he tried to fill a number of sensitive and prominent positions,
Clinton had been beset by a range of difficulties, stemming from the
miscalculations of his own administration and the resourcefulness
and opportunism of its critics. After being burned in the early months
of his presidency by the failed Justice Department nominations of
Zoë Baird as attorney general and Lani Guinier as head of the Justice
Department's civil rights division, Clinton was then startled by the
abrupt withdrawal under fire of his first choice to replace Les Aspin
as secretary of defense, Bobby Inman.[8] Drawing less attention from
the public and the press, but adding to the staffing problems of the
new president, conservative senators, often with the support of right-
wing lobbying groups, launched major attacks on no fewer than seven
other executive branch nominees, for posts ranging from the
Department of Defense to the National Endowment for the
Humanities, and succeeded in blocking two of them.

The impact of these setbacks was both practical and symbolic.
The withdrawal of Baird's nomination contributed to delays in staffing
Clinton's Department of Justice that dragged on well into the second year of his presidency. The withdrawal of Guinier's nomination's
undermined Clinton's relationship with two important sources of
political backing for any Democratic president—the civil rights community and the Congressional Black Caucus, whose defections on
the crime bill led to an embarrassing legislative setback which the
administration barely managed to reverse.[9]

Understandably made cautious by these and other controversies
over executive branch nominations early in his presidency, and eager
to avoid similar experiences with his Supreme Court nominations,
Clinton put his potential choices through a sort of public vetting process. This procedure first embarrassed them by making them targets
for critics and then left the impression that they were somehow want-
ing once they were selected. And by drawing out the process, Clinton

also added to the public impression that he was lacking in decisiveness and backbone. "He's like a windflower and goes in whichever direction the wind blows," complained University of Chicago law professor Philip Kurland.[10]

And ultimately, Clinton's choice of Judge Breyer for the Supreme Court and his selection last year of Ruth Bader Ginsburg to replace retiring Justice Byron White disappointed liberals who recalled Clinton's early talk of nominating Mario Cuomo, the epitome of liberal activism, or some other politician with "a big heart" as a counterweight to the unabashed conservatism of Justice Antonin Scalia and Chief Justice Rehnquist.[11]

Yet, given Clinton's ambitious legislative agenda, the determination of conservative lawmakers and interest groups, and the undependability of many in his own party, the president may well have felt he had no choice but to back away from a fight. To pick a nominee closer to the hearts of liberals, and to his own stated early intentions, would risk defeat, or at the least a jarring controversy that would add to the difficulties of stitching together the coalitions required to enact his program. "The important battles for Clinton are the ones he doesn't have to fight," said David Mason, Heritage Foundation specialist on congressional affairs and a former Reagan White House aide, referring to the necessity for Clinton to husband his resources to help push through legislation. "The problems he faces in the confirmation process have to influence his approach to the selection process."[12]

Not surprisingly, liberals and conservatives blame each other for the continuing conflict. Conservatives claim the liberals ignited the continuing wars over appointments by ganging up to block Ronald Reagan's nomination of Robert Bork in 1987, relying on what *Boston Globe* reporter Ethan Bronner in his book *Battle for Justice* described as "the masterly use of media manipulation and message framing."[13] But on the liberal side, Ralph Neas, executive director of the Leadership Conference on Civil Rights, a coalition of 185 national organizations, claims that "movement conservatives," as he calls them, escalated the struggle when Clinton took over the White House by opposing an unprecedented number of executive branch nominees.[14] And some people blame the media for distorting important, substantive issues for the sake of stirring controversy and attracting readers and viewers.

All these charges carry some measure of truth. But in fact the reasons for the turmoil run broader and deeper. In examining these factors, it is important not to mistake symptoms for causes. To understand the roots of the contentiousness over presidential appointments, it is necessary to take a long look back at the development of our political institutions, especially political parties.

The constitutional separation of powers makes the task of parties difficult, if not impossible, by ordaining a permanent antagonism between the executive and the legislature that often transcends party allegiance. This in effect creates a gap between politics, which is about what voters want, and government, which is what they get.

The parties have always had trouble filling this gap, but in the second half of the century, their failure has grown more dramatic and evident. This trend has had powerful impact on the presidency. The president's difficulties under the separation of powers are most evident when the Congress is controlled by the opposition party, a circumstance that has been increasingly common in recent years. But even when a majority of the Congress owes nominal allegiance to the same party as the president's, the separate constituencies and divergent interests of the legislators make it difficult for the president to rely on them for support. The situation, as Clinton's former chief of staff Lloyd Cutler has pointed out, is best summed up by the celebrated phrase of old-time fight manager Joe Jacobs: "It's every man for theirself."[15] This homely philosophy was much in evidence during Clinton's first two years in the White House, creating difficulties for him on appointments, and hamstringing his legislative efforts.

Unable to depend much on party support, and facing growing expectations from the enlargement of federal power, presidents have tended to personalize their office and their approach to government, relying heavily on new communications technology, particularly television. This tendency has further weakened the parties and made presidents less accountable. In the era of personalization, chief executives have sought to build constituencies and make policy decisions on their own, beyond the reach of parties and other institutions, and in the process contributed to the wounds inflicted on the presidency during the past generation—notably Vietnam, Watergate, and Iran-Contra. These and other misfortunes, including the inability of chief executives to match the hopes they had stirred in the electorate, have damaged presidential prestige and made them vulnerable to challenge on a range of issues, including major appointments to the executive and judicial branches.

Underlying the loss of party effectiveness, and the consequent weakening of the overall political system, are sweeping social, economic, and technological changes that have eroded old political loyalties. Americans have been on the move in several directions at once, from the Northeast and Midwest to the South and West, from the cities and rural areas to the burgeoning metropolitan suburbs, while the nation's old-line manufacturing base has declined and high-tech and service jobs have surged. Offsetting gains in civil rights for minorities has been a rise in ethnic and racial tensions, exacerbated by new influxes of immigrants of all colors and creeds. The traditional extended family has all but vanished, and the stability of today's nuclear family is threatened by a range of economic and social pressures.

Amidst this flux, the interests of individual Americans have become increasingly diverse and complex, covering a range of matters from abortion and crime to day care and health insurance, and thus increasingly likely to conflict with the concerns of their fellow citizens. The outcome for post-industrial America has been what sociologist Morris Janowitz labels the "disarticulation" of society: the splintering of traditional constituency groups into myriad fragments, leading to the spread of organized special interest groups on both left and right that have to some degree taken over the role parties used to play.[16] More than twenty million Americans belong to such groups and an additional twenty million give money to them, far more than contribute to the two major parties, an allegiance that makes it increasingly difficult for parties to count on their support.[17]

Interest groups have learned that confirmation battles can help advance and protect their objectives. "A lot of people ask why the battles were fought against (G. Harrold) Carswell and (Clement) Haynsworth," says Ralph Neas, recalling two unsuccessful nominations made by President Nixon. He claims that by blocking the nominations of Haynsworth and Carswell, the civil rights groups forced Nixon to nominate Harry Blackmun, "who became a revered figure in the progressive community," and Lewis Powell "who regularly voted to repudiate Meese and Reagan on civil rights cases." As for the more recent battle against Bork, Neas said: "We never would have gotten a (Justice David) Souter without the Bork fight, and many people would argue that (Justice Anthony) Kennedy is far better for us than Bork."

Just as interest groups have in part supplanted the role of the parties, so have the media, whose involvement in the political process has been shaped by technological and social forces. The biggest technological change is of course the advent of television, with its

ability to drown out the traditional channels of political communication that the political parties relied on in the past to maintain their
support. Television entered the appointment process twenty-five years
ago when it began airing confirmation hearings. While presidents
and other politicians often complain about the growing intrusiveness
and power of television, most have contributed to both trends by
exploiting television at every opportunity, often sacrificing their privacy to promote their images.

Television has also significantly influenced the print media; its
ability to deliver news almost simultaneously with the event has
spurred the tendency of the print press to provide more interpretive
coverage of the news rather than rely on the objective reporting that
was the staple of past years. As Tom Rosenstiel of the *Los Angeles Times*
has pointed out: "Newspapers feel compelled to provide context, perspective, and interpretation, since they infer that many of their audience are already familiar with the basic facts."[18]

But the power of television was not the only factor leading the
press toward taking a more subjective and usually more skeptical
stance toward the news. The series of national traumas mentioned
earlier, stemming from wrongdoing and deceit at the highest levels of
government starting with Vietnam and Watergate and extending to
Iran-Contra, has led journalists, along with the public at large, to be
more suspicious of political leaders, and to be more aggressive in
investigating them. "Many journalists are . . . determined not to
ignore or slight again what most deeply believe," writes former *New
York Times* correspondent Tom Wicker, "that they have a constitutional responsibility to inform the public about . . . corruption and
deceit."[19]

Some analysts, and some journalists, too, feel that the media
have carried this attitude too far. "The press is—and not just in its
coverage of national politics—far too inclined to report things which
go wrong, at the expense of the many which go right, and too
inclined to a cynical pose toward much of human motivation," writes
Everett Carll Ladd, head of the Roper Center for Public Opinion
Research.[20]

This criticism and other complaints often heard about the press's
overall coverage of public policy are also made about its performance
in dealing with the appointment process. Some scholars and politicians complain that reporters sometimes blow insignificant details
out of proportion, that they are subject to manipulation by foes or

champions of the nomination, and that the press appears to have no consistent standards for covering nominations. The critics also worry that all these defects are magnified by such new technological weapons as videotape and computerized access to library archives that heighten the opportunities for digging into the nominee's past.[21]

There are other basic realities about the press, an understanding of which helps to illuminate the media's role in the confirmation process. The most important is that, unlike the interest groups for whom confirmation fights are part of their reason for existence, the press's interest in whether a nominee gets confirmed or not is secondary to its interest in the news. Consequently, the press's role in the appointment process is almost always reactive, rather than proactive. On this point there is near unanimous agreement among those I interviewed, all of whom who have been either directly involved in the process or close observers for an extended period.

"The people who start the nominating fights are the people who don't want the person confirmed," said Karl Gawell, a lobbyist for the Wilderness Society who has been involved in the process as a Capitol Hill staffer and lobbyist for twenty years. "What the press does is like throwing logs on a fire that is already burning."[22]

"The press is really a conveyor belt, not an initiator," said Stephen Hess, a White House aide to Presidents Eisenhower and Nixon and now a Brookings Institution specialist on the Washington press corps. "If there is a controversy, usually it is the interest groups who start it, and once it starts, the press is going to cover it."[23]

Another reality is that while the world of media has changed greatly in recent years, these changes have had only limited impact on the appointment process. It is true that the trend toward televised confirmation hearings has dramatized some confirmation fights and heightened their impact on the public. But there is no conclusive evidence that the role of television, or other developments in the media—such as the birth of the Cable News Network (CNN), the spread of so-called tabloid television shows, and the proliferation of radio talk shows—have made confirmation fights more likely.

Looking back on the three major confirmation battles of the Reagan-Bush years—President Reagan's choice of Robert Bork for the Supreme Court, and President Bush's selections of former Texas senator John Tower to head the Pentagon, and of Clarence Thomas for the Supreme Court—it is hard to believe that these nominations would not have been opposed regardless of the media's role. Evidence that the contentiousness in the appointment process is shaped mainly by nonmedia forces comes from the numerous confirmation fights waged over the years over lower level appointments (see Chapters 4 and 5), which have gotten little if any media attention.

These battles reflect the combativeness of interest groups, and also the increasing aggressiveness of individual senators as a result of the decentralization of power in that body, forces that are totally independent of media influence. As G. Calvin Mackenzie, executive director of this Task Force, points out: "There is no effective way to stop miners and sappers like Jesse Helms (R-N.C.) or Howard Metzenbaum (D-Ohio) who too often see confirmation decisions as stages on which to act out their independent and often tangential policy concerns."[24]

In high profile confirmation fights where media involvement is significant, interest groups have adjusted their tactics to take advantage of the media spotlight. But these adjustments do not alter the basic strategic decision as to whether or not to contest a nomination. "We used to focus almost entirely on the print media," recalled Ralph Neas. "Then as I grew in this job and realized the impact of television we shifted to make sure the networks and C-SPAN had the facts."

Despite the complaints about media coverage from some critics, most interest group activists on both sides of the fence see the media simply as a conduit for the arguments of both sides, even when their side loses. "You could say that the press should do things differently," said David Keene, a former Nixon White House aide, now an adviser to Senate majority leader Robert Dole and chairman of the American Conservative Union, about the press's role in the battle over the Bork nomination. "But the fact is that press was there and Bork was there and the people against Bork were putting out stuff and what is the press supposed to do?"[25]

Ralph Neas thinks the media coverage on high-level nominations benefits the process. "You have top reporters and really significant analysis," from the print media he said. He also applauds the live television coverage of major confirmation hearings. "They are an extraordinary opportunity to get all the substantive issues out there."

Much of the criticism of the press is based on the belief that the press is too aggressive in covering the appointment process. But in view of widespread public cynicism about politics and government, I would argue that journalists have an obligation to scrutinize presidential nominees for high office, providing of course they are fair and accurate. Indeed, without such scrutiny, the media would have difficulty maintaining their own credibility. As Tom Rosenstiel notes in explaining the press's increased willingness to challenge the political establishment: "Today's more skeptical public would not be satisfied with the credulous coverages of the 1950s and 1960s when the quotes of public figures went unchallenged."[26]

The need for skeptical scrutiny in the appointment process is supported by mounting evidence bearing out Fred Wertheimer's contention that the Senate's own examination of the nominees is too often routine. Thus the *New York Times* reported in July 1994 that John H. Dalton had been confirmed as secretary of the Navy by lawmakers, most of whom were unaware of the fact that he had been accused of "gross negligence" in the management of a failed savings and loan.[27]

The problems of Housing and Urban Development Secretary Henry Cisneros were another apparent reason for anxiety about the thoroughness of the Senate's own investigations of nominees. It was disclosed that the Justice Department was considering opening an investigation into whether Cisneros told the full truth to the FBI about more than $250,000 he had paid to his former mistress in settling her lawsuit claiming that their love affair had damaged her career.[28]

Of course the press needs to observe the traditional rules that have governed the trade: get it first, but first get it right. And journalists should strive to carry on their task in a way that earns the respect and trust of the public. But if Americans sometimes are distressed about the press seeming indecorous, it should be kept in mind that by its nature our political process is a rough and tumble competition in which the press has its own unruly part to play. "A cantankerous press, an obstinate press, a ubiquitous press must be suffered by those in authority in order to preserve the even greater values of freedom of expression and the right of people to know," federal judge Murray Gurfein wrote in the *Pentagon Papers* case: "There is no greater safety valve for discontent and cynicism about the affairs of government than freedom of expression in any form."[29]

While the role of the media in the appointment process is important, extravagant attention to this single factor amounts to what Professor Charles Jones, University of Wisconsin presidential scholar and author of *The Presidency in a Separated System*, calls a "cop-out."[30] Along with most of those I interviewed he believes there are other more fundamental explanations for the turmoil in the appointment process—particularly divided party government. Indeed, if there is

one point on which Democrats and Republicans, liberals and conservatives agree, it is that the inherent weaknesses of the political system
that have fostered contentiousness over presidential appointments have
been greatly compounded by the split-level political and governing
system that developed in the 1970s and 1980s. In other words, divided
government was not only a significant consequence of the defects in
the political system, it made these defects worse. This was made plain
during President Clinton's first two years in the White House, when his
ability to exploit the anticipated advantages of united government was
crippled in large part because of factors resulting from the period of
divided government. One such element was the heightened partisanship among congressional Republicans, who sought to stymie him at
every turn, and another was the assertiveness of his own party's members on Capitol Hill, which made them resistant to his leadership.

In the wake of the return of divided government, as a result of
the 1994 midterm elections, it is important to understand the development of the problems that afflicted the appointment process during the previous two years of Democratic control of Congress and
the White House. Starting in 1969, for a period of nearly a quarter of
a century, it was said that the Democrats could not win the White
House while the Republicans could win nothing else.[31] With the
Republicans maintaining control of the White House, the Democratic
party became the party of the legislative branch, wielding what power
it could through increasingly extensive use of advise and consent.
"Some of us had doubts about this," recalled Mark Gitenstein, longtime chief counsel of the Senate Judiciary Committee under Senator
Joseph Biden.[32] "We wanted to see Democrats take back the executive
branch some day, and we also could see how this would come back to
haunt us. We stretched the limits of this to the utmost."

Republican David Keene also attributes contentiousness to the
longtime split in government that heightened antagonism between
the two parties. This hostility has persisted, as President Clinton has
discovered, even after divided government ended:

> In the past there was always the feeling that the presidency
> would someday change hands and there was always this gen-
> tlemen's agreement that, "There but for the grace of God go
> I," and that if you mistreat this president's nominee the
> other guys might mistreat yours. But that broke down in the
> eighties. That resulted, first, in Democrats going after the

Republican nominees when they couldn't get Reagan. Then, when Democrats took over the White House, Republicans decided they were going to do exactly the same thing. And it's one of those things that is hard to call a halt to. It's an endless circle of internecine warfare.[33]

The result, as President Clinton learned only too well, was a level of political guerilla warfare that used to end on election day but no longer does. Confirmation fights have become part of what Benjamin Ginsberg and Martin Shefter have described as the era of "post-electoral" politics.[34] They wrote that, as a consequence of the decline of parties and stalemate in the political arena, "contending political forces have come to rely upon such weapons of institutional combat as congressional investigations, media revelations, judicial proceedings and alliances with foreign governments."

Fights over presidential appointments have thus become surrogates for political campaigns, taking on all the excesses that define modern campaigning. As Fred Wertheimer notes:

If you look at this appointment phenomenon, you can see that is the same phenomenon we all have watched in politics and governing and in the way the press goes about covering politics and governing. Everything is campaign mode oriented. We get into techniques and approaches that are used in electoral politics—newspaper ads, charges and counter charges, hot rhetoric, very negative, lots of attacks, lots of personal stuff, lots of "beat up the other guy."

The intensity of feeling is reflected by Ralph Neas's explanation of how, in 1981, he came to join the Leadership Conference on Civil Rights, the major liberal alliance in the civil rights field. A former legislative assistant to liberal Senate Republicans, Neas was considering whether to practice law or take a post with the civil rights group when he was given some advice by a fellow Notre Dame graduate, John Sears, one of the architects of the campaign that had just propelled Ronald Reagan into the White House. "There are only so many opportunities to be part of history," Sears told Neas. "And my friends in the Reagan Administration are now going to try to undermine everything that you and the Leadership Conference have ever done. And you should be involved in that battle."

The current politicization of the appointment process began with the struggle for ideological control of the Supreme Court that has been waged, with intermittent truces, for most of the past thirty years. On that, left and right both agree. For it was the judicial activism of the Court, spurred by the inadequate response of the other two branches of government to such problems as racial discrimination, that energized a range of interest groups. In these skirmishes, they sharpened their teeth and refined the skills that they would then put to use in battles over executive branch appointments.

Paul Weyrich, who as head of the Free Congress Foundation functions as the sort of panjandrum of right-wing interest groups, traces much of the contentiousness to Lyndon Johnson's attempt to appoint Abe Fortas chief justice of the Supreme Court, a move that was blocked by a Republican filibuster. Weyrich says,

> That particular episode really embittered the Democrats because they had overwhelming control of the Senate. They felt their party wasn't able to exercise its will because of a small minority. They were then determined to get the nominations Nixon made. That's when the politicization of the process really began and it has just continued to ratchet up every couple of years, whoever is in power.[35]

It was these battles over judicial nominations that drew press attention to the presidential appointment process. "The appointment process is an extension of politics into other arenas," said Ken Bode, professor of communications at DePauw University and moderator of public television's *Washington Week in Review*, "and the press is the vehicle for all this."[36] This pattern was dramatized, Bode recalled, by the 1987 struggle over Judge Bork's nomination to the Supreme Court, which was touched off by Massachusetts Senator Edward Kennedy's hyperbolic attack on Bork. Bode noted:

> Kennedy gives a speech the very day he's nominated which ratchets through the media. He gets the word out and he politicizes the nomination and the appointment process. It has become so deeply politicized that every time there is a vulnerable nominee there is always a reason to pay the other guy back for the last one. And we play it like a big story. Which it is.

2

THE CUTTING EDGE

The turbulence that has marked the appointment process in recent decades is in marked contrast to the relative placidity that prevailed for the first two thirds of this century. This harmony held true for appointments to both the executive branch and the judicial branch that served as the forcing ground for confirmation controversy.[1] In fact, not until Harlan Fiske Stone in 1925 was a Supreme Court nominee even called upon to testify before the Senate in this century; he was easily confirmed.[2]

This noncontentiousness was sustained even during the New Deal. Despite Franklin Roosevelt's controversial economic reforms, the still strong tradition of party loyalty shielded his nominations to the executive branch. As for the judiciary, though the Supreme Court's resistance to FDR's policies led to the historic battle over his court-packing scheme, this friction only rarely spilled over into the process of selecting the eight justices Roosevelt picked, more than any president since George Washington. The most heated controversy stemmed from the nomination of Alabama senator Hugo Black, a hard-driving Southern progressive who had endeared himself to FDR by his support for the court-packing scheme.[3] After Black was confirmed by the Senate in August 1937, but before he was sworn in as a justice, the *Pittsburgh Post Gazette* reported that he had been a member of the Ku Klux Klan before his election to the Senate more than a decade before.

In the face of the public uproar, Black responded to the attack by one branch of the media by defending himself on another—the radio. He admitted joining the Klan but said he had quit when he ran for the Senate and had nothing more to do with it. In today's political and press environment, it is hard to imagine that hard evidence of Black's membership in the Klan, which was rumored when Roosevelt first submitted his name to the Senate, would not have been unearthed and publicized prior to the Senate vote confirming his nomination. Moreover, it might have been much harder today for him to withstand the storm of protest that would certainly follow the news. As it was, since Black was already confirmed, his foes, though not mollified by Black's radio address, could do nothing but call upon him to resign—a demand he refused. He was sworn in October 4, 1937, a date described by his foes as "Black Day," and took his seat on the Court where for more than twenty-five years he served as a bulwark against the bigotry that the Klan represented.

Still, the episode left a significant legacy. The American Bar Association recommended that the Senate Judiciary Committee henceforth conduct public hearings on judicial appointments. And less than two years later, when FDR sent Harvard professor Felix Frankfurter's name to the Senate, his nomination was referred to the Judiciary Committee for hearings on his fitness.

Like Black, Frankfurter was probably fortunate not to have been nominated three decades later. His was a controversial nomination. He was Jewish, and there was already one Jew on the Court, Justice Louis Brandeis. And conservatives also complained about his "radical" background as a champion of the anarchists Sacco and Vanzetti, whose murder conviction in a Massachusetts payroll robbery was a great liberal cause celebre during the 1920s. Misgivings were so widespread that, on the day his nomination was announced, Brandeis received an ominous telegram from his friend, Groucho Marx: "Congratulations," the comedian wired. "If confirmed please send autographed photo."[4] But with the help of Dean Acheson, who served as his counsel, Frankfurter glided through the committee hearings and was confirmed by a voice vote of the Senate.[5]

For the rest of the Roosevelt years and the Truman presidency that followed, the nomination process was relatively tranquil. It was during the Eisenhower presidency that trouble began to stir, with the nomination of California governor Earl Warren as chief justice. Warren himself was confirmed with relatively little difficulty. But as the Court over which he presided created a furor with rulings overturning racial segregation, expanding the rights of criminal suspects, and banning school prayer, Court nominations edged closer to the political arena. A series of skirmishes foretold the greater battles ahead.

In November 1954, Eisenhower nominated John Marshall Harlan, whose grandfather had made a lasting reputation for himself for his dissent from the separate-but-equal doctrine of *Plessy v. Ferguson.* That same month the Democrats regained the Senate majority they had lost in Eisenhower's 1952 election, and arch segregationist Democrat James Eastland of Mississippi chaired the Judiciary Committee when Harlan appeared for his confirmation hearing. Fearful that Harlan would be as opposed to segregation as his grandfather, Eastland heckled the nominee on the issue of race so relentlessly that Eisenhower felt compelled to personally apologize to Harlan after he was ultimately confirmed.[6]

The next Eisenhower appointment, William J. Brennan, had his confirmation postponed even longer, for five months, as a result of procedural delays contrived by Senator Joseph McCarthy. Then in the twilight of his notorious career, McCarthy remained powerful enough to postpone Brennan's confirmation because the new justice had once likened McCarthy's investigations to the "Salem witch hunts."[7] Eisenhower's last Court appointee, Judge Potter Stewart, had to wait more than six months for confirmation when senators demanded to know whether he thought the Constitution meant the same thing in 1959 as it had meant in 1787 and whether he accepted the reasoning of the integration decisions.

All this was "symptomatic of a smoldering discontent with the developing trends of constitutional decision."[8] It continued to smolder for most of the next decade, in large measure because when the Democrats recaptured the White House in 1960 behind John Kennedy, divided government ended. Kennedy's two Court nominees, Byron White and Arthur Goldberg, were relatively circumspect. And party loyalty helped avoid serious attacks from Southerners even though both nominees predictably added to the Court's majority in favor of integration.[9] Much the same gentle treatment was accorded Abe Fortas when Kennedy's successor Lyndon Johnson nominated him to the Court in 1965.

Meanwhile, resentment of the Warren Court intensified, as evidenced by the confirmation of Johnson's next nominee, Thurgood Marshall. The nomination was heavily tinged by politics. Johnson was eager to appoint a black to the Court.

He wanted the historical recognition and, more practically in summer 1967, with the country torn by black rioting in urban areas, Johnson hoped to ease racial tensions. But Marshall's nomination had political significance for Southerners, too, not only because of his race but also because he could be counted on to strengthen the liberal majority on the Court.

At any rate, the Southerners on the committee bullyragged him at length. "Thurgood Marshall was subjected to a degree of racist smear that the confirmation process had not seen before and has not seen since," claimed Yale law professor Stephen Carter. But the Senate finally confirmed him by a 69 to 11 vote.[10] But there was no television in the hearing room, by the long-standing edict of Chairman Eastland. And coverage by the print press was relatively undramatic, reflecting the perception that Marshall would eventually be easily confirmed, as indeed he was, and that his Southern foes were mostly going through the motions of attacking him to satisfy those among their constituents embittered by the many recent advances of the civil rights revolution. "The embarrassing truth is that the campaign that failed in 1967 might have succeeded a quarter of a century later," Carter contended.[11]

But that speculation seems farfetched, given Marshall's stature and the prevailing public sympathy toward the cause he symbolized. Indeed, Fred Graham, who covered the hearings for the *New York Times* and is now managing editor of cable television's *Court TV* thinks that if the hearings had been televised, the result might have been to restrain Marshall's foes on the committee and benefit the nominee. "People might have gotten down on the Southerners," he said. "They made themselves pretty unattractive."[12]

3

POLARIZATION

Even as the Senate cast the ballots that confirmed Marshall, the setting for the appointment process was undergoing a dramatic change because of two major developments—the political backlash against the Warren Court and the decline in presidential authority. For more than a decade the Court had been under attack for its "activism"; from one side reckless demagogues stirred popular indignation against the impact of its decisions, while on the other side high-minded scholars complained that in their anxiety to achieve a desired result, the justices had been careless about the Constitution and judicial precedent. In any case, the activism of the Court in plunging into the partisan thicket reflected the paralysis of the established political institutions. The Court had acted in the final analysis because the legislatures, both state and national, and the political parties had failed to act, particularly on the issue of race, which Gunnar Myrdal had called "The American Dilemma." And so the Court found itself in what was fast becoming an untenable position. As James F. Simon put it in his chronicle of the turmoil surrounding the Supreme Court:

> And so the Warren Court had become the cutting edge for
> national reform in the second half of the twentieth century,
> attacking America's number one social problem, racism,
> rooting out rural bias in state legislatures and giving America's
> pariahs—police suspects as well as political mavericks—an
> opportunity to be heard.[1]

   This was about the last thing Americans wanted in 1968, a time
when racial antagonisms and frustration with the war in Vietnam were
boiling over into violence in the nation's cities and uprisings on its
campuses. At a time when most middle class Americans wanted reas-
surance about their institutions, the Warren Court challenged them.
A dismayed Walter Lippmann called the United States "the most vio-
lently disordered" of the world's developed nations; to restore "discipline authority and self reliance," Lippmann called for the election of
Richard Nixon.[2]
   Nixon heard the knock of opportunity. To signal to voters the
new tone of strength he would bring to the presidency and presumably the Court, Nixon did what no presidential candidate had done in
modern times: he made the Court and its decisions a campaign issue
and a target, something even FDR had refrained from doing in 1936
when he was frustrated by decisions handed down by the "Nine Old
Men." In keeping with his campaign theme of law and order, Nixon
attacked the Court's criminal law opinions. Reeling off bloodcurdling
examples of murder and rape, he charged that the Court had caused
a "weakening of the peace forces as against the criminal forces in this
country."[3]
   On civil rights, Nixon was more subtle, wary of alienating supporters in the north. But speaking to Southern delegates at the
Republican convention earlier in the year about Court efforts to end
school desegregation, he had declared: "I know there are a lot of
smart judges. But I don't think there is any court in this country
including the Supreme Court of the United States that is qualified to
be a local school district and make the decision as your local school
board."[4]
   Nixon's rhetoric had to be taken seriously because his chances of
winning the White House were being increased by the conflict over
the Vietnam War that was tearing the Democratic party that year.
Johnson had taken himself out of the race, and his chosen successor
Vice President Hubert Humphrey was having a hard time rallying
Democrats behind him. That meant Johnson had to face the strong
possibility that Richard Nixon would succeed him in the White House.
   That also meant that Nixon stood a good chance of making the
selection that would fill the vacancy that would be left when seventy-
seven-year-old Chief Justice Warren retired. Warren did not like the
idea that his successor might be chosen by Richard Nixon, who had
allied himself with the views of the Court's bitterest foes. Johnson

and Warren had a better idea: an end run around the normal func-
tioning of the political process.[5]

After conferring with Johnson, the chief justice announced that
he planned to retire but did not set a certain date. Instead, he said
that he was prepared to stay on in his present post until Johnson wanted him to leave. Johnson quickly decided on replacing Warren with
his longtime adviser Abe Fortas, whom he had appointed to the Court
three years earlier. That created yet another vacancy, which he decided to fill with another old friend, Court of Appeals judge Homer
Thornberry. And the open-ended way Warren had worded his resignation gave Johnson an additional advantage in pushing the Fortas
nomination through. If Senate conservatives balked at confirming
Fortas, they would be stuck with the much reviled Warren at the helm
of the Court for an indefinite time to come.

If Johnson carried off this scheme, as Republicans were quick to
complain, he would in effect take away from their candidate for president one of the prizes of the office he was seeking—the right to
appoint a chief justice. Johnson's answer to such criticism was to point
out that seven other Supreme Court justices had been appointed by
presidents in their last year in the White House and had been confirmed. He did not bother to mention that nine others nominated
under similar circumstances had failed to win confirmation.

At any rate, Johnson was confident that he had lined up the necessary backing in the Senate. He believed he had promises of support from James Eastland of Mississippi, the Judiciary Committee
chairman; Richard Russell of Georgia, leader of the Southern bloc;
and Everett Dirksen of Illinois, the Republican Senate leader. Despite
his well-deserved reputation as a master political strategist, two factors
Johnson did not fully understand undermined his plans.

First, Johnson did not comprehend the extent to which his own
authority as chief executive had been diminished—by his status as a
lame duck and by the damage to his popularity and credibility from
his conduct of the war in Vietnam. And his failure to grasp that reality, as reflected by his effort to promote Fortas, further diminished his
prestige. Second, Johnson also failed to grasp the changes in the
Senate as an institution. In the two decades after World War II, when
Johnson made his mark on the Senate, it had been "an insulated and
conservative institution" dominated by a few senior members. The
appointment process, like the outcome of most legislation, was pre-
dictable.[6] By the late 1960s, though, with the general weakening of

established political leadership and of party allegiance, new senators, even relatively junior members of the body, felt free to flex their muscles and to take advantage of political opportunity. The old influence of the Senate leadership and of the White House had been eroded by the new boldness of individual senators. They sometimes found support from the fast emerging interest groups but they also had their own resources— expanded staffs that served their own offices and the committees of which they were members. "If you bring a bunch of bright young people to town anxious to do a job and increase their resumes then sure as shooting they are going to go out and work at it," points out Charles Jones of the University of Wisconsin.

The new dynamics of the Senate turned the Fortas nomination, which Johnson conceived of as the final master stroke of his presidency, into a disaster. All the Senate giants whom Johnson had aligned on the side of the nomination were confounded by a very junior Republican, Robert Griffin of Michigan, who had been in office little more than two years. Griffin lined up eighteen Republicans to oppose the nomination on the grounds that a lame duck Democrat should not make an appointment that might well go to a newly elected Republican chief executive. He also quietly allied himself with Richard Russell and his Southerners, who were eager to take the chance to prevent the liberalism of the Warren Court from being perpetuated.[7]

The bipartisan anti-Fortas coalition was able to mount a filibuster against the nomination until it received a final blow. This was the disclosure that Fortas had accepted a $15,000 fee for conducting a series of seminars that summer at American University, with the money coming from five wealthy businessmen with far-flung interests, three of whom were clients of Fortas's old law firm. In the wake of that disclosure and the questions it raised about Fortas's ethical standards, hope of ending the filibuster died and Fortas asked that his name be withdrawn.

The failure of the nomination not only was a blow to Johnson's prestige, but to the authority of the office he held and passed on to Richard Nixon. The success of Griffin's rebellion and his ability to create a bipartisan alliance against the nomination left individual senators with a new awareness of their potential for striking out against established political leadership. More directly, the damage to Fortas's reputation, because of the questionable propriety of the American University fee, left him vulnerable to new attacks on ethical grounds.

Eight months after his inability to win confirmation as chief justice, and six months after the election of Richard Nixon, Fortas was in effect deconfirmed from his post as associate justice. The immediate reason was the disclosure by *Life* magazine that he had accepted a $20,000 fee from a charitable foundation run by Louis Wolfson, a freewheeling financier who was ultimately convicted of violating the federal securities laws. Later it was revealed that Fortas's contract with the foundation called for him to be paid $20,000 a year for life. But Fortas had returned the money and canceled the arrangement when he learned that Wolfson faced criminal prosecution.

Few people had much to say in Fortas's defense, and the American Bar Association found his conduct to be "clearly contrary" to the canons of judicial ethics. But even some of Fortas's critics were disturbed about the role that the Nixon administration's Justice Department had played in aggressively investigating Fortas's conduct and in leaking negative information about the case to the press and the Senate.[8] University of Chicago professor Philip Kurland described these actions as the "removal" of a justice by "extraconstitutional means."[9]

It soon became clear that the political struggle for the Court that had begun with Lyndon Johnson's nomination of Fortas to be chief justice was only beginning.[10] One factor that contributed to the conflict was divided government. Nixon's 1968 election had left the Senate in Democratic hands. Not only that, but Nixon's own party in the Senate was divided, between conservatives opposed to the civil rights rulings of the Warren Court and civil rights liberals who backed the drive to desegregate.

In August 1969, when Nixon selected Fortas's replacement— Clement Haynsworth, chief judge of the Fourth Circuit Court of Appeals—liberals viewed the nomination as part of Nixon's so-called Southern strategy, to weaken the Supreme Court's strong stand on civil rights in order to gain Southern votes. They fought the nomination. Just as important, so did the AFL-CIO, angered by Haynsworth's decisions on labor cases favoring the textile industry that the unions were desperately trying to organize. Haynsworth thus faced the opposition of two of the most powerful and best organized interest groups in the Democratic party—labor and civil rights.

But their influence would not have been sufficient to defeat him without the issue of ethics, on which organized labor focused early, complaining of Haynsworth's financial interest in a vending machine company that did substantial business with a textile firm that had been helped by a controversial court ruling in which Haynsworth had joined. Labor was helped by a story by William Eaton, then of the *Chicago Daily News*, detailing Haynsworth's involvement with the vending machine company. Eaton's story won a Pulitzer prize. But it was only part of the evidence unearthed by Senate liberals and the AFL-CIO during their look into Haynsworth's extensive stock holdings, which fostered the impression that the judge had been insensitive to conflicts of interest and the appearance of impropriety.

Haynsworth's foes seized upon the ethics issue because they doubted they could defeat the nomination on grounds of philosophy. The view that the president had a constitutional right to pick a Supreme Court nominee who conformed to his own beliefs still held sway, though it was steadily losing ground. Moreover, a fair number of senators shared Haynsworth's views on civil rights and labor law, or at least did not disagree enough to oppose his nomination. Furthermore, the ethical questions about Haynsworth took on extra weight because of the circumstances that forced Fortas off the Court. "Will the same Senators and commentators who demanded the purity of one judge demand it also of another?" asked Stephen Schlossberg, general counsel of the United Auto Workers, of the Senate Judiciary Committee. The answer inevitably had to be yes. Haynsworth was defeated by a vote of 55 to 45, with 17 Republicans joining 38 Democrats. It was the first defeat of a Supreme Court nominee since 1930.

On his second attempt to fill Fortas's seat, Nixon again turned to the South and selected Federal Circuit judge George Harrold Carswell of Florida. Though Carswell's financial affairs presented no problem, civil rights forces viewed his record in that area as even more repugnant than Haynsworth's. Once again the media played a significant role. Ed Roeder, a Florida television reporter, unearthed from the files of a defunct small town Georgia paper a twenty-year-old speech in which Carswell affirmed his undying belief in racial segregation and white supremacy (demonstrating in that pre-Nexis-Lexis era that journalistic enterprise and legwork is more important than technology). As the fight raged in the Senate, Bill Wise, a press aide to Indiana senator Birch Bayh who was leading the anti-Carswell forces, tapped into the resources of the national magazines, big city newspapers, and television networks. "I arranged to give them all tips we got and they ran down ten blind alleys for every payoff" he said.[11] But the interest groups contributed as much as the press. A researcher for the Washington Research Project's Action Council, a civil rights organization, probing Carswell's activities in Florida, found that he had signed the incorporation papers transforming the public golf course in Tallahassee into a private club so that it could continue to operate on a segregated basis.

Two other developments in the Carswell case had long-term significance. Unlike the controversy over Haynsworth, whose foes considered his philosophy out of bounds, Carswell's critics went after him on the grounds of his judicial philosophy. They were bolstered by an influential article in the *Yale Law Journal* by Professor Charles Black who argued that a senator had not only a right but a duty to vote against a Court nominee whose views, "when transposed into judicial decisions, are likely in the Senator's judgment to be very bad for the country."[12] Black's argument found more senators receptive in the case of Carswell than of Haynsworth, in part because Carswell's views seemed more extreme than Haynsworth's, and also because by nominating Carswell after Haynsworth's defeat, Nixon provided more evidence of his determination to politicize the Court, in effect almost daring those who disagreed with him to oppose him.

Still another breakthrough was on the issue of competence, a subjective standard that the Senate almost never sought to impose in the past, even when confronted by mediocre choices. Lewis Pollak, dean of the Yale law school, told the Judiciary Committee that Carswell "presented more slender credentials than any nominee for the Supreme Court put forth in this century."[13] And over five hundred professionals from ten government agencies signed a petition calling on the Senate to reject Carswell because of his "utter lack of qualifications as a jurist."[14] But this issue is remembered less for the criticism of Carswell than for the defense offered by Nebraska senator Roman Hruska, who said, "Even if he were mediocre, there are a lot of mediocre judges and people and lawyers. They are entitled to a little representation, aren't they?"[15]

The Senate decided otherwise, voting 51 to 45 against mediocrity and Carswell, with 13 Republicans in opposition. Nixon delivered a bitter tirade against the Senate. He had concluded, he said, that "with the Senate presently constituted I cannot nominate to the Supreme Court any Federal appellate judge who believes as I do in the strict construction of the Constitution." For good measure, he accused Carswell's foes of "regional discrimination" and "malicious character assassination."[16]

Following that battle, Nixon nominated and the Senate readily confirmed as Fortas's replacement Circuit judge Harry Blackmun, who was from Minnesota, like Nixon's newly appointed Chief Justice Warren Burger. In September 1971, two more vacancies occurred. Three potential Nixon nominees came under fire and Nixon was forced to drop them from consideration. In the end he finally appointed a Southerner, Lewis Powell of Virginia, and nominated William Rehnquist, head of the Justice Department's Office of Legal Counsel, to the Supreme Court. Liberals concentrated their attack on Rehnquist for his civil liberties and civil rights views, but the respect held even by his critics for his intellect and legal scholarship stood him in good stead. He was confirmed, although twenty-six senators voted against him.

This concluded one of the most jarring chapters in the history of the Court. In less than three years, one justice was forced to quit, and two designated replacements were rejected by the Senate. Three other prospects had to be discarded. And Rehnquist's nomination provoked the largest vote against a successful Supreme Court candidate since Charles Evans Hughes was confirmed as chief justice in 1930.[17]

By their actions, both Johnson and Nixon undermined the credibility of the presidency and made it more respectable to challenge presidential nominations. The grounds for challenging nominations had been broadened to include ethical and ideological considerations as well as the question of competence. Just as important, the media had emerged as a factor to be reckoned with in the appointment process. The press became involved in confirmation fights because the choices made by the presidents and the response of interest groups and senators had made these proceedings into a political battlefield.

To be sure, the symbiotic relationship between journalists, interest groups, and Senate staffers that had begun during the Haynsworth and Carswell confirmation fights continued. Often it operated much as Bill Wise of Bayh's staff described it: reporters got leads from legislators and interest groups and tried to check them out. But the impact of all this was limited. Most journalists were properly skeptical of such leads and only a few of them produced significant revelations. Of course, reporters also pursued leads on their own. But even when these did produce relevant information, the outcome of confirmation fights continued to be shaped by more fundamental political forces as I came to understand from firsthand experience. During the battle over Rehnquist's nomination, which I covered for *Newsweek*, I learned from a disinterested and trustworthy source that in 1953, when Rehnquist was a law clerk to Justice Robert Jackson, he had written a memo on the historic case of *Brown v. Board of Education,* then before the Court. The memo urged that Jackson uphold the separate-but-equal doctrine of *Plessy v. Ferguson* rather than find segregation to be unconstitutional. As history has noted, Jackson voted the other way, as did all the other justices. When *Newsweek* published the memo, it created a minor sensation. But it was late in the game; Rehnquist had already won the grudging approval of the Senate Judiciary Committee. When I got to the Senate press gallery on the day the full Senate voted to confirm Rehnquist, James Flug, a staffer working for Senator Kennedy, who opposed the nomination, asked me rather plaintively, "What else have you got for us?"

This incident helps to illustrate how the press's role in the confirmation process usually works in reality. Neither Flug nor anyone else in the Senate or in any of the interest groups involved in the nomination battle had anything to do with my story. I reported the story and *Newsweek* published it in the belief that it provided information relevant to Rehnquist's qualifications for the Court. But it turned out that the impact of the story was overridden by other factors. Rehnquist was a conservative but he was no bigot like Carswell, nor was he mediocre. And anyhow, the Senate had already made up its mind.

4

FORD AND CARTER:
LULL BETWEEN STORMS

Following the struggle over Rehnquist, the guns of the appointment process fell relatively silent for more than a decade, covering the end of one presidency, that of Richard Nixon, the duration of two others, Carter's and Ford's, and lasting into the beginning of a fourth, Reagan's. But the forces of contentiousness that had been generated by the political tensions of the Johnson and Nixon era did not evaporate. They only became temporarily less conspicuous because of circumstances in the overall political environment; when these changed, the disputes would be revived. Indeed, even during this comparatively calm time, there were enough clashes and controversies, particularly in the lower levels of the executive branch, to demonstrate the fundamental potential for conflict in the appointment process. As previously noted, the media had only limited involvement in these fights because most of the positions at stake were relatively obscure. The print press recorded them in routine fashion and television paid even less attention.

Among the reasons for the lull that prevailed for most high-level appointments: there was only one Supreme Court vacancy during this period, and Gerald Ford filled it with a moderate federal judge, John Stevens, who provoked little controversy. As to the executive branch, Nixon had talked of revamping his entire administration at the beginning of the second term. But he was forced to abandon those plans when he was engulfed by the Watergate scandal, so he gave the Senate few chances to oppose his nominations. When Ford abruptly replaced Nixon, he faced continued Democratic control of the Senate. He tended to stand pat with the incumbent appointees at the cabinet level at first. And when he eventually replaced members of the Nixon cabinet, he was careful to pick well-established and well-respected figures who for the most part were able to avoid the sort of controversies that could hurt efforts to rehabilitate the Republican party and the presidency in the wake of Watergate.

Ford had good reason for caution, as demonstrated by the reaction to his most significant appointment, that of former New York governor Nelson Rockefeller to fill the vice presidential vacancy created by Ford's ascension to the presidency. The choice of Rockefeller, made under the Twenty-fifth Amendment to the Constitution, which had been used only the year before by Nixon to make Ford vice president, at first was greeted with wide acclaim. But then disclosures that Rockefeller had made gifts of more than $2 million to associates prominent in public affairs, including Secretary of State Henry Kissinger, aroused controversy over Rockefeller's motives. Four months after his nomination, and after he had promised to put his financial holdings into a blind trust, Rockefeller was finally confirmed. Though an angry Ford blamed "partisan politics" for the delay, the episode appeared mainly to reflect the post-Watergate atmosphere of suspicion toward all politicians and intensified scrutiny of their personal finances.[1]

That same attitude, along with the growing willingness to challenge the president's appointments on a range of grounds, which also was intensified by Watergate, contributed to the opposition met by some of Ford's subcabinet appointments. Thus in 1974 he was forced to withdraw the nomination of Andrew E. Gibson to the Federal Energy Administration after it was disclosed that Gibson had been promised $880,000 in severance pay from his former employer—an oil company.[2] Similarly, Ford gave up plans to nominate former Nixon White House aide Peter M. Flanigan to be ambassador to Spain because of charges that Flanigan had been involved in providing ambassadorial appointments in return for big contributions to Nixon's infamous 1972 reelection campaign.[3]

In 1975, Ford's second year in the White House, ideology entered into the opposition to some of his subcabinet nominations. Ultraconservative brewery executive Joseph Coors was turned down for a post as board member of the Corporation for

Public Broadcasting in part because senators said they feared he might attempt to censor public television programs. Foes also contended that Coors would have a conflict of interest because he served on the board of Television News Inc., a family-owned enterprise that distributed news reports to subscriber stations. Similarly, Ben Blackburn was rejected as chairman of the Federal Home Loan Bank Board because as a Georgia congressman he had voted against the 1968 Fair Housing Act.[4]

In the presidential election year of 1976, when Ford had to face a challenge to his nomination from Ronald Reagan before confronting Democratic standard bearer Jimmy Carter in the fall, politics served to complicate the appointment process. The Senate rejected Ford's choice of New Hampshire Republican leader (and later senator) Warren Rudman to chair the Interstate Commerce Commission, which was announced early in February not long before the New Hampshire presidential primary in which Ford was being challenged by Reagan. Ford's critics in both parties claimed the appointment had been made to boost Ford's chances in New Hampshire. And Ford's nomination of George Bush, who had been Republican national chairman as well as envoy to Peking, as head of the Central Intelligence Agency was confirmed only after Ford publicly pledged that he would not select Bush as his running mate in 1976.[5]

Election-year pressures also provided another example of the deconfirmation process. The victim was agriculture secretary Earl Butz, who at the height of the fall campaign stirred a storm of criticism after a joke he had told that was both racist and lewd was published. Ford tried hard to hang on to Butz, whose farm policies he regarded as an asset to his administration, but was forced to ask for his resignation to avoid damage to his candidacy from the controversy.[6]

Jimmy Carter's election in 1976 brought an end to the period of divided government, but its effects lingered on. As a self-proclaimed political moderate, Carter seemed unlikely to stir ideological controversy over his nominations. Yet even he had trouble early in his presidency, in part because during the eight years of Nixon and Ford, senators from his own party had grown used to challenging the White House and going their own way.

Carter's major problems as he set out to staff his presidency stemmed from two nominations in the national security area. In the wake of disclosures about nefarious activities by the Central Intelligence Agency in the previous two decades, President-Elect Carter chose an outsider, former Kennedy White House aide Theodore Sorensen, to head the Central Intelligence Agency.

The intelligence community, a powerful but normally almost invisible interest group, made its opposition felt immediately. The attack, sometimes coming from anonymous sources, on the nominee of a newly elected chief executive just as he was about to begin his anticipated honeymoon period, defied precedent and was another measure of the increasing vulnerability of the once almost sacrosanct nominating authority of presidents. Senate conservatives complained that Sorensen lacked experience in intelligence and raised other issues that they contended made him a poor choice. Carter called the attacks on Sorensen "groundless and unfair," but three days before the inauguration, Sorensen asked that his nomination be withdrawn.[7]

Carter's next serious problem came with the nomination of Paul Warnke to be chief U.S. Arms negotiator. Warnke was regarded as too dovish in his approach to the Soviets by many in the Senate, including influential Democrats. Aiding the fight against Warnke was a newly organized interest group, the Committee on the Present Danger, whose members included such prominent foreign policy hardliners as Dean Rusk and Eugene Rostow. Though Warnke did win confirmation, forty senators voted against his nomination. This negative vote served as a warning to Carter that the hawks in the Senate had the power to prevent ratification of the new arms control treaty with the Soviet Union that Carter was seeking to negotiate.[8]

Carter also had to endure an example of the deconfirmation process, triggered by ethics issues similar to those that had been raised in the Johnson and Nixon eras. His longtime adviser Bert Lance was forced to resign his post as head of the Office of Management and Budget because of charges of impropriety about his activities as a banker in his home state of Georgia.[9]

In sum, the Ford-Carter lull was a reminder of the continued vulnerability of the presidency to attacks on appointees and even on incumbent officeholders. The battlegrounds were no longer limited to the Supreme Court and civil rights. Instead, they spread to the executive branch and to national security issues.

5

REAGAN:
REPOLARIZATION

With the election of Ronald Reagan, the polarized politics that had marked the end of the Johnson presidency and the Nixon presidency would return with a vengeance. But this did not happen immediately. At first, fights over high-level appointments were few. With Reagan's landslide victory, the Republicans had gained control of the Senate for the first time since 1958, making it easier for the president to gain approval of his nominees. Then, too, liberals were demoralized and in disarray as a result of the 1980 election returns. And finally, Reagan himself helped to avoid a possible controversy with his first nomination for the court, made in his first year as president. Redeeming a campaign promise to put a woman on the high court, he selected Sandra Day O'Connor, an Arizona judge known as moderate conservative. She was confirmed by the Senate in a vote of 99 to 0.

Three of Reagan's early executive branch appointments aroused controversy. All were confirmed, but as it turned out, all three ended their cabinet careers on a negative note. Alexander Haig's appointment as secretary of state created a stir because of his previous role as chief of staff in the Nixon White House. He was confirmed after thirty hours of hearings for a post which he resigned after a year because of policy conflicts within the White House.

James G. Watt, confirmed as secretary of the interior despite bitter opposition from environmentalists, also ultimately resigned. But unlike Haig, Watt was forced out of office. Like Abe Fortas and Bert Lance, he became a victim of the "deconfirmation process." Watt's performance at the Department of the Interior, particularly his determination to open vast amounts of federal land for energy exploration and commercial enterprise, had confirmed the worst fears of the environmentalists. But their criticism was to no avail. Then, in 1983, Watt described the membership of an advisory commission he had established as composed of "every kind of mix you can have. I have a black, a woman, two Jews and a cripple." The resultant furor forced his resignation and underlined a reality of the politics of confirmation and deconfirmation. As Brooks Yeager, a former lobbyist for the Sierra Club, remarked: "When he was nominated we opposed him on policy grounds and couldn't get anywhere. But he makes one dumb crack and he's finished."[1]

The final controversial cabinet nominee was Reagan's choice as labor secretary, Raymond J. Donovan, whose confirmation was held up because of allegations that his New Jersey construction firm was linked to organized crime. He won Senate approval following an FBI probe that could not substantiate any of these charges. But in 1985, Donovan resigned after he became the first sitting cabinet member in history to be indicted; along with other members of his firm, he was charged with fraud and grand larceny supposedly committed before he joined the cabinet. He was acquitted in 1987.[2]

Meanwhile, at the subcabinet level, even though his party controlled the Senate, as a result of the continuing surge in independence by individual senators and the accelerating fragmentation of both parties, Reagan found that some of his nominees had to face opposition from across the political spectrum, from Republicans as well as Democrats. In 1981, backers of human rights from both parties on the Foreign Relations Committee forced Reagan to withdraw his nomination of Ernest W. Lefever as assistant secretary of state for human rights, citing Lefever's past opposition to President Carter's human rights policies. This was the first time in recent memory that this committee had rejected a presidential nominee.[3]

Reagan's attempts to appoint conservatives on the domestic side were set back by a bipartisan group of senators in 1982. The president withdrew his nominations of nine members of Legal Services Corporation's board of directors after fifty-two senators signed a letter saying they would not support three of his choices. Reagan had tried to abolish the Legal Services Corporation, established to give legal aid to the poor, when he first took office, and critics claimed he had chosen the three controversial nominees for the board in hopes they would restrict the agency's activities. The White House said some of the other six nominees withdrawn were not "philosophically in tune" with Reagan's policies.[4]

Reagan also had to face conservative opposition to some of his appointments, particularly in foreign policy, mainly due to the efforts of North Carolina's hawkish right-wing senator, Jesse Helms, a master of the parliamentary maneuver. In 1982, opposition led by Helms forced Reagan to withdraw the nominations of Robert T. Grey, Jr. as deputy director of the Arms Control and Disarmament Agency and Norman Terrell as director of the agency's Bureau of Nuclear Weapons control. Helms and his allies objected to the record of the nominees on arms control in past administrations but also used the nominations to challenge the Reagan administration's approach to arms control talks with the Soviet Union. The threat of a filibuster by Helms also forced Reagan to shelve the nomination of Richard Burt to be assistant secretary of state for European affairs. Helms objected to articles Burt had written while he was a reporter for the *New York Times*.[5] Burt was eventually confirmed to that post. But in 1985, when Reagan named Burt ambassador to West Germany, Helms, contending that Burt was too eager to reach a nuclear arms pact with the Soviet Union, held up his nomination and the nominations of twenty-eight others named to ambassadorships and other foreign policy positions. The administration finally got Helms to yield by promising to find foreign policy posts for four conservatives supported by Helms and his allies.[6]

But most of the opposition to Reagan's appointments, as to his policies as president, came from liberals, not conservatives. The longer Reagan stayed in office, the more resentful liberals became of his policies. Unable to make much headway with legislation, they found an opportunity to strike back in the appointment process in the fourth year of Reagan's presidency when Reagan picked White House counsel Edwin Meese III to fill a vacancy as attorney general.

Liberals launched a two-pronged attack. Taking a rare stand against an executive branch appointment, the Leadership Conference on Civil Rights claimed that the "extreme" positions taken by the Reagan White House on civil rights showed that Meese would not vigorously enforce the civil rights laws as head of the Justice Department.[7] But this line of attack was hard to pursue, because it depended on inference rather than fact.

More troublesome to Meese were charges of unethical conduct brought by another interest group, Common Cause, based on the contention that he had helped get federal jobs for persons who had given him financial assistance.[8]

Following more than a year of public debate and after an investigation by an independent counsel cleared him of criminal charges, Meese was confirmed by the Senate in February of 1985, by a 63 to 31 vote, as Reagan began his second term.

That vote was enough to give encouragement to Reagan's foes among the interest groups and in the Senate. In June 1985, they launched another attack at a Justice Department nominee. This time the target was William Bradford Reynolds, the head of the civil rights division, whom Reagan sought to promote to the post of associate attorney general. Speaking for the Leadership Conference, Ralph Neas told the Senate Judiciary Committee that Reynolds's record at the civil rights division was "a disgrace," charging that he had repeatedly ignored the intent of Congress when it passed civil rights laws and defied the rulings of the Supreme Court.[9] Even more damaging to Reynolds were contradictions between his version of events and the statements of other witnesses and contradictory information from documents provided by his own department.[10] By a ten to eight vote, with two Republicans joining eight Democrats, the committee voted against reporting Reynolds's nomination to the floor.

But liberals had less success the next year when Warren Burger resigned as chief justice. Reagan nominated Rehnquist, by far the most conservative of the sitting justices, to take his place. Reagan also chose appeals court judge Antonin M. Scalia, just as conservative, and just as brilliant as Rehnquist, to take Rehnquist's position as associate justice. Civil rights groups launched a massive attack on Rehnquist while providing only nominal opposition against Scalia. "It was a strategic decision," Ralph Neas explained. "With Republicans in charge of the Senate and two Supreme Court nominees, if you went after both you had no chance of defeating either. But if you focused on Rehnquist and defeated him there would be no spot for Scalia."

Among other arguments, the NAACP Legal Defense and Education Fund contended that of eighty-three civil rights cases in which he had participated, Rehnquist had voted against the civil rights plaintiffs eighty-two times. It was disclosed that property Rehnquist owned had restrictive racial and religious covenants. But with the

Republicans still in control of the Senate, the civil rights forces had to be content with getting thirty-three negative votes on the nomination, the most ever cast against a Supreme Court nominee who was confirmed.

Even with the two new conservative appointments, the Court remained in a precarious battle between right and left. It was clear to both sides that the next appointment would see a renewal in the long struggle for the Court. Setting the stage for that battle was the success scored by Democrats in the 1986 elections when they regained control of the U.S. Senate by a 55 to 45 margin. Apart from the psychological boost, the election results gave Democrats an advantage they had lacked for six years in battles over appointments—control of the Senate and its procedures.

The new balance of power in the Senate was soon tested when Supreme Court justice Lewis Powell announced his retirement in June 1987. He had functioned as the ideological middleman on a sharply divided Court. By filling the Powell vacancy with a true conservative, Reagan would be able to shift the course of American jurisprudence to starboard for many years to come. The obvious choice was Judge Robert Bork of the U.S. Circuit Court of Appeals, a man possessed of both unquestioned conservative beliefs and intellectual powers acknowledged even by his enemies.

Civil rights forces and other liberal interest groups girded for battle. But Delaware senator Joseph Biden, newly installed as chairman of the Judiciary Committee, wanted to avoid a contest in the Senate that might interfere with his own bid for the Democratic presidential nomination. "Joe said to me, 'I don't want a fight on this,'" recalls Mark Gitenstein, then his chief counsel. "'I want to go out and campaign in Iowa.'"[11]

Under orders from Biden, Gitenstein urged Howard Baker, who had taken over as White House chief of staff in the wake of the Iran-Contra revelations, not to select Bork for the Powell vacancy, but instead to pick a moderate whom Democrats could support. Baker passed the word to the president—who nevertheless made Bork his choice. "I think the White House decided that because of Iran-Contra they needed a victory to rally the right wingers," Gitenstein said.

"We thought he could be confirmed," said David Mason, then a White House aide. "We had no negative experience with him," he added, pointing out that Bork had won Senate confirmation as solicitor general and then as circuit court of appeals judge. But the stakes were much higher now, nothing less than control of the Court, and the liberals put up a much tougher fight than they ever had before.

To a degree they drew on the lessons of past victories. Thus, as with Carswell, the target was Bork's philosophy, although unlike the critiques of Carswell, liberals did not challenge Bork's competence. But perhaps more significantly the liberals drew on the lessons from their past defeats by conservatives in using the media to shape public opinion.[12]

"We learned during the Reagan years that the White House and the movement conservatives knew how to frame the debate," Ralph Neas told me recently. "They had sophisticated techniques to define issues. For four or five years we were relegated to the second to last paragraph of stories. But by 1985 and 1986 we started to frame the debate and catch up with them."

Indeed, by the time of the Bork battle in 1987, there was evidence that the liberal groups had not only caught up but passed their right-wing enemies. To mobilize support against Bork, the liberals used polling and focus groups, targeted ads at the constituencies of fence-sitting senators, flooded the print media with op-ed pieces, and produced an unending stream of point-persons to argue their case on radio and television talk shows. While such shows had been around for years, the liberals had come to realize they were taking on increasing importance as outlets for one side or another in controversies over public policy.[13]

And when it came to appealing to the public's emotions, few efforts by the conservatives could match the raw impact of the opening statement by Massachusetts senator Edward M. Kennedy in attacking Bork in which he charged that: "Robert Bork's America is a land in which women would be forced into back alley abortions, blacks would sit at segregated lunch counters, rogue police would break down citizens' doors."[14]

What the liberals succeeded in doing was what the conservatives had accomplished before: they swamped the media. "Everybody reported the speech," wrote Ethan Bronner of the *Boston Globe*, noting that Kennedy's hyperbolic rhetoric amounted to a distortion of what could be reasonably inferred from Bork's record. "The more sophisticated news organizations made clear that it was unusually sharp, pointing to the partisan nature of the looming battle." But even columnists who later criticized the Kennedy attack as irresponsible did so only in sweeping terms without specifically analyzing the basis of the charges.[15]

Bronner took a similarly dim view of the paid advertising campaign against Bork. He wrote:

> Half truths are the most effective tools of the advertiser. It was partly through such advertising that liberal packagers constructed an image of Robert Bork. . . . They took Bork's own words and decisions and pared away subtleties, complications and shadings. What remained was neither lie nor truth. It was half truth. Like the half-truths of the Reagan years it played well.[16]

The main hole in the argument that Bork, who lost his confirmation fight by a 52 to 48 Senate vote, was done in by foul blows is the reality that Bork was his own worst enemy. When the hearings began, polls showed that the public was about evenly divided for and against Bork's confirmation. After he had testified, the nays were ahead by eight to ten points.[17] As Ralph Neas said: "Media helped. But Robert Bork defeated Robert Bork."[18] While it is hard to prove such distinctions, polls after the hearings indicated that only 24 percent of the public saw television advertisements dealing with the nomination while 60 percent claimed to have seen part of the hearings on television.[19] Reagan ultimately filled Powell's vacancy by appointing another federal appeals judge, Anthony Kennedy, also a conservative, but by most measurements more moderate than Bork. He easily won confirmation, but his appointment gave liberals reason to feel that their fight against Bork had not been for naught. But if the Bork battle was a liberal victory, it was also a lesson for conservatives from which they would profit.

6

BUSH:

PREEMPTIVE STRIKE

Though George Bush had won the White House by using against Democrat Michael Dukakis an escalated version of the tactics Bork's liberal critics had used against the judge's nomination, once in office, Bush called for a political truce, and promised to lead Americans into the "kinder and gentler" future he had first adumbrated in his speech accepting the Republican party's presidential nomination. But his election had done nothing to bolster the authority of the presidency or heal the divisions within the political system, both of which contributed importantly to the contentiousness in the nominating process. Moreover, the election left the Democrats in firm control of the Senate, in position to take advantage of these factors. And before his presidency was a month old, this reality was brought home to Bush with a rude jolt when his nomination of former Texas senator John Tower to be defense secretary turned into a battle royal—and for Bush a battle lost.

The Senate rejected Tower's nomination by a 53 to 47 vote, almost entirely on party lines. It was only the ninth time in history the Senate had turned down a cabinet nominee, the second time that it had rejected one of its former members, and the first time it had refused to confirm a president's cabinet nomination made at the start of his term.[1]

To a large extent, Tower was of course a victim of divided government. In addition though, the circumstances that resulted in the Democratic majority voting almost solidly against him underlined how closely linked the appointments process had become to political debate. The most damaging ammunition Tower gave his critics stemmed from his apparent inability to satisfy two criteria—ethics and morality. Some critics of the appointments process claim that these are merely examples of gimmicks or "hooks" used to trap nominees and defeat them. But the issues of ethics and morality that dominated much of the debate about Tower's nomination did not come out of a vacuum. Rather, they had become an important part of the rhetoric of American politics and it was only natural that Tower's foes would seize upon them to use against him.

Ethics had been a major issue since Watergate. And Bush himself had unwittingly added to Tower's vulnerability by his emphasis on ethics early in his presidency, an apparent attempt to distinguish his administration from that of Ronald Reagan, which Democrats had denounced as a citadel of sleaze. Bush appointed a special commission to "take a fresh look" at existing ethical standards for all three branches of government, urging public servants to "bend over backwards to see that there's not even a perception of conflict of interest."[2]

It soon became clear from Tower's own testimony that this was not the way Tower had operated in the consulting work he had been doing for defense firms. He acknowledged receiving more than $750,000 from big defense firms between April 1986, when he left government service as arms control negotiator and December 1988, when he quit his consulting activities because he was under consideration for the Pentagon post. Democrats voiced their suspicions that the companies were actually paying Tower not for his advice but for favors rendered when he served in the Senate and for influence he would wield in the Pentagon.

Perhaps even more troublesome for Tower, because it was more emotional, was the issue of morality. Once again Bush had contributed to the salience of this issue by his emphasis on "traditional family values" in his campaign against Dukakis. In addition to what Bush had to say on this subject, the issue had been underlined by a range of right-wing groups allied with the Republican party and supportive of the Bush candidacy.

It was one of the most prominent leaders on the right, conservative activist Paul M. Weyrich, who thrust the issue of morality directly into the Tower confirmation hearings. Weyrich told the Senate Armed Services Committee that as a result of having on several occasions seen Tower drunk and making advances to women other than his wife, he had "serious reservations" about Tower's moral character. Because of Weyrich's credentials as a staunch conservative, his criticism of Tower's behavior opened the way for critics from elsewhere on the political spectrum to pursue this subject, and Tower's personal life soon became the focus of a wide range of allegations, some of which, his supporters contended, had no basis in fact.

"What I did was create a certain climate which permitted all sorts of people to speak out who have other problems with him," Weyrich told me at the time.[3] His analysis of the impact of his testimony underlined the complexity of political relationships that had come to dominate the appointment process when the right circumstances were present.

> Most of the objections were raised because people had their own agendas and Tower was seen as interfering with them. I think there were a couple of Senators who had genuine concerns about what I said. (James) Exon of Nebraska was one of them. And the chairman, Sam Nunn (of Georgia) was another. Beyond that the people who stepped forward and postured one way or another were generally people who either didn't like Tower because they thought he was too conservative or didn't like him because he advocated one particular defense program over a program they preferred or because they had other candidates for the job in mind.

Weyrich's own motives are subject to varying interpretations that point up the sometimes Byzantine nature of the politics of presidential appointments. In the explanation he offered me at the time, he depicted himself as simply trying to raise the alarm about a potential danger to national security.

> My concern was with the national security implications of a guy who has some very serious personal problems. Because in my opinion with Tower it's not a question of a guy who maybe had an affair with his secretary and slips off the straight and narrow. I'm talking about a guy who in my opinion has a reprobate mindset. When somebody has a problem they subject themselves to enormous pressures.

But other conservatives detected less altruistic reasons for Weyrich's testimony against Tower. "I think this was an example of somebody doing something to make himself more important," said David Keene. "He was looking for somebody he could kill off to show he had clout. That was a conscious decision." When I asked Keene why he believed this, he said: "Because that's what everybody close to him says was the reason for what he did."

Whatever Weyrich's motives, Tower was vulnerable to the morality issue Weyrich raised as well as the ethics issue, in part because of another factor that is important in political combat: the ex-senator's personal standing among his peers. His arrogant manner had left him few friends among those with whom he served who normally would have been expected to support his nomination. "Tower was not well liked by his fellow senators," David Mason, who had left the White House to take a post at the Pentagon where he had expected to serve under Tower, told me recently. "He was not a member of the club."

When it came to making his first nomination to the Supreme Court, Bush still enjoyed the high public approval ratings provided by the success of Operation Desert Storm, and he made certain to avoid spoiling his favorable image by setting off another appointment controversy. To fill the vacancy created by the resignation of Justice William Brennan, the Court's most effective liberal, in summer 1991 Bush named a newly minted circuit court judge, David Souter. A scholarly, relatively obscure figure who lived an almost monastic life, Souter had left such a meager record of his beliefs, particularly on such controversial issues as the Court's 1973 *Roe v. Wade* ruling upholding the right to abortion, that he was called "the stealth candidate." The mystery left both conservatives and liberals uneasy, but it also gave no one sufficient ammunition to attack him. He won Senate confirmation by a 90 to 9 vote.

But by the time the next vacancy on the Court occurred, in fall 1991, circumstances were different. First of all, the vacancy was created by the resignation of Thurgood Marshall, the Court's only black justice. To fill that post by appointing a white male would lend ammunition to the oft made Democratic charge that Bush, whose opinion poll ratings had been driven down by the recession, was insensitive to the rights of minorities. Bush found a way to blunt that criticism and also satisfy Republican right wingers whose support he wanted to solidify for the approaching presidential election. He nominated a conservative federal appeals judge named Clarence Thomas, a black with strong conservative credentials.

When reporters, noting Bush's vehement opposition to racial quotas, asked if he was not in effect contradicting himself by picking a black judge to fill the vacancy left by a black judge, Bush indignantly declared: "What I did is look for the best man. The fact that he is a black and a minority had nothing to do with this."[4]

Given Thomas's insubstantial record of legal achievement, that judgment seemed implausible on its face. But the press and Thomas's liberal critics had a hard time proving this, even after the American Bar Association's rating committee gave him only a modest "qualified" rating, the lowest rating given to any Court nominee since Carswell in 1970.[5] Bush had painted liberal interest groups who had brought down Bork into a corner. "On civil rights issues Judge Thomas is closer to Ed Meese than Thurgood Marshall," contended Arthur Kropp, president of People for the American Way.[6] President Bush has opted for ideological purity instead of an open minded vision of justice," said Nan Aron, head of the Alliance for Justice. But the ranking Republican on the Senate Judiciary Committee, Orrin Hatch of Utah, pointed to Thomas's humble roots in the rural south. "Anybody who takes him on in the area of civil rights is taking on the son of a sharecropper," Hatch said.[7]

This was just the point the White House and right-wing interest groups sought to drive home. On the day that Thomas's nomination was announced, the national press corps was briefed by the White House on Thomas's "extraordinary life, his rise from poverty to power."[8] And the White House stressed the same theme in the list of "talking points" it distributed to Republicans who were counted on to boost Thomas's cause. Even the picturesque name of Thomas's hometown, Pin Point, Georgia, where reporters from national media rushed to chronicle Thomas's life, helped to dramatize the Horatio Alger image Thomas's supporters sought to evoke.

As for the right-wing interest groups, still smarting from the defeat of Bork, they decided they would not be caught off guard by the liberal interest groups again. They launched a preemptive strike, only instead of attacking a nominee as the left had done with Bork, they were defending one, depicting him as a sort of folk hero who had risen to the top of the heap, depending not on liberal programs or handouts but his own fortitude and ambition in the American tradition of self-reliance.[9] Pat Robertson's Christian Coalition spent more than $1 million on Thomas's behalf, including an ad which showed Thomas in front of the American flag.

Along with building up Thomas, the right-wing groups also attacked Thomas's foes. Gary Bauer, head of the Family Research Council, an organization stressing traditional values, organized the Citizens Committee to Confirm Clarence Thomas and raised $500,000 for a print and television ad campaign. One commercial accused Thomas's critics of mudslinging, literally showing mud being thrown at Thomas's face. The massive outlays for advertising heightened the similarity between confirmation fights and political campaigns. But judging from the polling after the Bork hearings (see end of Chapter 4) it is questionable whether any amount of advertising could match the impact of the hearings carried free on television.

Meanwhile, the liberals were struggling to catch up. They had been prepared for Bork, but not for Thomas. And they found it difficult to campaign against a black with Thomas's personal background. "Thomas's supporters framed the debate, based on the Pin Point Georgia strategy and that gave them a head start," Ralph Neas told me. "And we did not get a consensus on opposing him until five weeks after the nomination. "Horatio Alger was an American hero, not a heavy," said David Kusnet, the liberal advertising consultant who explained why the themes used against Bork could not work against Thomas.[10]

Not only did Thomas appear to be an authentic American hero, he was an *African*-American hero. Civil rights forces opposing Bork had been able to gain support of Southern Democrats by warning them that if they supported Bork they would alienate black voters. But it was difficult to make that case against Thomas, because his race shielded him against attacks on his civil rights stands.

Yet even with the liberals in disarray, Thomas's idiosyncratic views on some issues, which committee chairman Biden called part of "an ultraconservative agenda," and his seeming disingenuousness in avoiding discussion of his beliefs on abortion kept him from winning a majority of the judiciary committee.[11] The best he could get was a tie, with seven of the eight Democrats opposing him and the eighth, Arizona's Dennis DeConcini, joining with the six Republicans in support of the nomination.

In announcing the vote, Chairman Biden declared that in considering the nomination: "I believe there are certain things that are not an issue at all. And this is his character, or characterization of his character." If Thomas's character should become an issue, during the subsequent Senate floor debate on the nomination, Biden said, "I have assured Judge Thomas and assure my colleagues I will be an advocate of Thomas's position."[12]

What Biden was talking about in those elliptical phrases was an allegation against Thomas about which few people outside the Judiciary Committee or the Bush White House even knew. But this charge would reach a much wider audience and for a time change the nature of the hearings.

Within a few days of the tie vote, the mystery surrounding Biden's statement was lifted when two reporters, Nina Totenberg of National Public Radio and Timothy M. Phelps of *Newsday* revealed to the world the shocking accusations by a University of Oklahoma law professor, Anita Hill. Going back a period of ten years, Hill charged that, when she had worked for Thomas first at the U.S. Department of Education, then at the Equal Employment Opportunity Commission, he had subjected her to sexual harassment.[13]

The charge of sexual harassment immediately commanded the nation's attention. But there was another disturbing dimension to the revelations—that the Senate Judiciary Committee had known of the allegations and chosen not to deal with them publicly. Thus not only were the reputations of Hill and Thomas, who immediately denied the charges, called into question. So also was the judgment and fairness of the committee members, all of them, as was pointed out innumerable times, white males.

The fact that the committee members knew of Hill's allegations might never have come out in the more sedate world of past confirmation hearings, but then again, none of this might have happened in the past. When James Eastland chaired the Judiciary Committee and Thurgood Marshall, the black justice Thomas replaced was up for confirmation, Eastland did not allow television cameras in the hearing room. And, looking back on the Haynsworth battle of 1969, Bill Eaton recalls that Judge Haynsworth had been through a messy divorce.

> We decided not to get into it. We thought it was not relevant. I thought that was the right decision at the time. Nowadays I think the pressure would be too great not to pick up the divorce.

Clearly standards are different now. Back in the 1960s, who knows what it would have taken to get Anita Hill or any other woman in her position to come forward with charges of sexual harassment? A consideration of the Thomas case suggests that the causes of increasing contentiousness of the confirmation process go well beyond changes in the media, not only to changes in our political process, but in our culture and our values that the media coverage reflects.

Inevitably, the hearings were reopened and a Senate vote delayed until their conclusion. For the next three days and nights, while millions of Americans watched with fascination, Hill and Thomas, at times descending to a level of prurience rarely reached in the Senate, let alone on network television, steadfastly stuck to their stories—she the allegation, he the denial. But Thomas had certain political factors on his side. One was his race, and the other was that, if the senators now accepted Hill's charges, after previously deciding not to investigate them, they would be passing judgment on themselves.

Then too, senators can never forget that they live in glass houses. Two members of the committee were particularly vulnerable on any matter related to personal behavior—Biden because of the plagiarism in his past that had forced him to abandon his 1988 presidential candidacy, and Kennedy, because of past indiscretions that included, most recently, his behavior earlier in the year at the family estate in Palm Beach in connection with an incident that led to charges of rape against his nephew, William Kennedy Smith. This left the normally aggressive Massachusetts senator in poor position to press Thomas about allegations of sexual harassment. Under no such handicap, several of the Republican senators enthusiastically browbeat Hill during the course of their cross-examination while the Democrats did little to shield her.

It was no wonder that the polls showed most Americans believed Thomas's version of events rather than Hill's.[14] Under the circumstances, the end result was inevitable. The Senate voted 52 to 48 to confirm Thomas. It was the largest negative vote against a nominee in this century. But regardless of the margin, Bush had consolidated the conservative control of the Court.

For the left it was a lesson that the tactics that liberals had used from Carswell and Haynsworth to Rehnquist and Bork could be turned against them. But one group on the left, the feminist organizations, found consolation. While they had lost a battle, they gained in Anita Hill a martyr who would help them boost their funds and their political fortunes for the next battle.

But to infer from this that interest groups stage confirmation fights mainly to raise money or boost their prestige would be an over-simplification. The commitment of the interest groups to confirmation fights is hard to separate from their basic reason for existence. "Does a group oppose Bork because they don't like Bork or because they want to promote themselves and raise money?" asked David Keene. "The two things are intertwined." Any conservative group with an interest in the Supreme Court was in effect obliged to go to bat for Clarence Thomas; similarly, any feminist group that wanted to maintain a reputation for militancy would have been under pressure to oppose Thomas and to stand up for Anita Hill. At any rate, it is not necessary to distinguish the various motives of interest groups, one from another, to conclude that the expansion of their numbers and influence, and the corresponding decline in the strength of parties, has been a potent factor in fostering the increasing contentiousness in the presidential appointments process.

7

CLINTON:

NANNYGATE AND BEYOND

The 1992 election that installed Bill Clinton in the Oval Office also restored the executive branch and the Senate to one-party control for the first time since 1980. Even so, the new president faced a host of problems as he contemplated staffing his government. A dozen years of Republican presidents had left Democrats on Capitol Hill outwardly pleased at their party's return to the White House, but unaccustomed to sharing authority for establishing their party's positions with the White House, and even more balky than they had been when Jimmy Carter assumed the presidency after eight years of GOP rule. After their long stretch in the political wilderness, Democratic interest groups were eager to get their hands on the executive branch's levers of power.

Clinton's vulnerability to challenge was enhanced from the outset by his lack of a majority in the popular vote and by uneasiness about his character stemming from the controversies about his personal behavior that had plagued his campaign. Polling continuously demonstrated that a significant portion of the electorate had doubts about Clinton's trustworthiness. More recent polls also indicated that these misgivings persisted during Clinton's first two years in the White House, partly as a result of new allegations made against him and partly as a result of sustained criticism that as chief executive he was too willing to cut corners and shift positions for political advantage. Many analysts offered this public wariness about the president's personal style as explanation for his relatively low approval ratings in the polls, given the improvement in the economy and his intensive efforts to deal with the economy and other domestic issues.

However, this unfavorable perception of Clinton needs to be understood in the context of the various national traumas cited earlier, which have been attributed by many to personal defects in our recent presidents. Critics have blamed Vietnam and Watergate on the overweening ambition and deviousness of Johnson and Nixon. The skyrocketing inflation that marked the presidency of Jimmy Carter has been attributed to his ineptitude, and even the immensely popular Reagan was lambasted for his laziness and unwillingness to accept responsibility because of Iran-Contra. All this has made citizens, and of course the media, more alert to apparent presidential foibles and more prone to judge presidents harshly on these grounds.

An inevitable consequence has been to contribute to the tarnishing of presidential prestige and shrinking of presidential authority that affects nearly every aspect of the office, certainly not excepting the power to appoint. "The public, the press, other politicians, and even interest groups tended to be more deferential toward presidents in the past," says Terry Eastland, former Justice Department information officer during the Reagan years and now editor of *Forbes Media Critic*. "Now there's less deference and more people are willing to take on presidential nominees."[1]

Forced to operate within this unfortunate zeitgeist, Clinton added to his difficulties by promising during the campaign to appoint an administration as variegated as the country itself, or as he put it, one that "looks like America." Inevitably this boosted the already high expectations of the various Democratic interest groups for prizes the appointment process offered, and made them more aggressive in claiming what they felt was coming to them.

In trying to keep his pledge, Clinton at times found himself caught in a crossfire between rival constituencies. Early in the transition period, he considered New Mexico congressman Bill Richardson a likely choice for the Interior Department. That would have pleased Hispanics. But it would have upset environmentalists already uneasy about Richardson's record on Western lands. Their first choice was Bruce Babbitt, who had a lifelong commitment to preserving nature but was a white Anglo-Saxon male. The environmentalists found a way out of that impasse. "We told Clinton that if he appointed Babbitt at Interior we would find another Hispanic for the cabinet," one member of the transition team explained.[2] And this was how former Denver mayor Federico Pena got to be secretary of transportation.

At times Clinton found the constituency group pressures on the selection process irritating. At a press conference a month before his inauguration, he scolded feminist groups for pressuring him to pick women, likening them to "bean counters" whom he accused of playing "quota games."[3]

Nevertheless, some critics suggested that it was Clinton's determination to pick women for top jobs that contributed to the first of a series of setbacks that plagued the appointment process in his first year in the White House. This was the selection of Zoë Baird, the former general counsel of Aetna Life and Casualty, to be attorney general. Baird's downfall, caused by the disclosure that she and her husband, Paul Gerwitz, a law professor, had hired an illegal alien as a baby sitter and failed to pay the required Social Security and unemployment taxes demonstrated the potential power of the media, and the public, to dominate the appointment process once the president loses control. When Baird's nomination was announced, the *New York Times* hailed her as the "most impressive" of a group Clinton had announced that day and columnist Anthony Lewis called her "an inspired choice."[4] Women were pleased to see a female in the top job at justice, even if she was not a member of the feminist cadre. Ralph Nader, suspicious of Baird's corporate background, announced his opposition, but he was almost alone in the field. In ideological terms, her nomination aroused no opposition either on the left or right, and her confirmation was considered all but certain.[5]

Meanwhile, though, Baird had disclosed her nanny problem to transition aides and had been advised not to worry about it. The decision was made to provide this information to the FBI as part of the background check it makes of all nominees, but to avoid public disclosure of the information for as long as possible. Judiciary Committee chairman Biden and ranking Republican Hatch were also informed, leaving it up to them whether to disclose this information before or during the confirmation hearings. This strategy seems to have ignored the possibility of a leak, a remarkably naive judgment considering the Bush administration's experience with the Clarence Thomas hearings little more than a year before.

Sure enough, the nanny problem was revealed on the front page of the *New York Times* only a few days before the hearing began, based on information believed by those close to Baird to have come from the

FBI.[6] Even after the initial public disclosure, few politicians saw the nanny problem as a bar to her confirmation. In fact, Republican Judiciary Committee members Hatch and Alan Simpson, of Wyoming, who had authored the law Baird violated, both predicted her confirmation, as did Democratic chairman Biden. But the *Times* and the *Washington Post* weighed in with tough editorials challenging Baird's fitness for the job.[7] And seizing upon the disclosure to bolster his attacks on Baird's nomination, Ralph Nader made himself almost a perpetual guest on talk shows, about sixty by his own estimate.

More fundamentally, "nannygate," as it inevitably came to be dubbed, took on a life of its own, fanned by talk shows all over the nation, the instruments of "electronic populism." Ironically, it was these shows that Clinton had used during his presidential campaign because he felt the conventional press was too preoccupied with the personal controversies that dogged his candidacy.[8] Now these programs on radio and television, carried by local stations in every community across the land, contributed to the undoing of his attorney general designate.

If these shows did not create the public indignation over nannygate, they amplified it, in a way that had never been experienced in the past when such shows had not been so eager to exploit political controversies. As Bill Eaton, now Capitol Hill correspondent for the *Los Angeles Times*, contended.

> This was a case in which the press was behind the curve. Most of the conventional wisdom here in Washington was that she (Baird) was going to fly, that all she had was a little problem of illegal immigrants. It wasn't the press that got on her case, it was the country. The talk shows were stirred up by the country. This all took place in about one day.[9]

The sense of public indignation expressed over the airwaves had little connection to ideology or partisan loyalty. "At least 75 percent of the callers say that she should step aside and most of them identify themselves as Democrats," said Michael Jackson, a widely listened-to talk show host on Los Angeles's KABC.[10] Many said they were infuriated because the disclosures about Baird appeared to contravene Clinton's promise, reminiscent of Bush's early pledges, that he wanted a government free from even the suspicion of impropriety. Moreover, while talk shows often have been blamed for whipping up public fury, in this case the anger appeared self generating and self perpetuating. At KSTP in Minneapolis, host Joe Soucheray said that after several straight days of the Baird furor, he wanted to change the subject, but the flood of calls continued to be "hot and heavy." The controversy really touched a chord in Boston, said Marjorie Clapprood, talk show host on WHDH. "Two thirds of the calls were from women who had been through the rigorous process of finding day care—and they were having none of it."[11]

And it wasn't just the talk shows that were getting phone calls from irate citizens about an attorney general candidate who had broken the law and had not paid her taxes. So also were the senators who grilled Baird at her televised confirmation hearings. "The calls are running fifty no, zero yes," crusty Howard Metzenbaum, Democrat of Ohio, told her as she testified. A few days later, Baird withdrew her name from consideration.

Who was to blame? Writing in the *American Lawyer*, Stuart Taylor argued that Baird's offense was "monstrously caricatured" by the talk shows and the press.

> What never got through in all the press attention is that in hiring their nanny Gerwitz (who was primarily responsible) and Baird were snared by a legal regime of mind-boggling irrationality and internal contradictions, run by a government that had a settled practice of not enforcing its own law against employing illegal aliens as domestics.

But to prepare his critique it took Taylor himself nearly 10,000 words and several weeks to sort out all these complications, which the press and television had to deal with under deadline pressure. And even at that, in an article based on interviews with sources sympathetic to Baird and her husband, Taylor himself concluded that Baird should never have been chosen for the job because she was "unfit for the symbolic role of ultimate champion of the rule of law."

Other analysts put the main responsibility for Zoë Baird's ordeal on the new president and his transition team. David Broder likened Clinton's choice of Baird to Bush's selection of Dan Quayle to be his vice president.

> Both let the choice slide until they were up against a deadline. Both insisted on great secrecy. Both made the decision

in isolation from their most experienced and reliable political advisers. And both let one arbitrary criterion override all the other standards they should have used. Bush wanted a baby boomer on the ticket. . . . Clinton limited his attorney general search to women. . . . No greater folly could threaten any president than falling into the habit of talking to the people . . . but not listening. That's the lesson Clinton should have learned from the Baird affair. If he didn't, watch out.[12]

But if any lessons had been learned from the Zoë Baird nomination, they were not apparent a few months later when another Clinton nominee at the Department of Justice ran into a buzz saw—Lani Guinier, his candidate for head of the civil rights division. As with Baird, Guinier faced a problem at the outset that the White House failed to take seriously enough, soon enough. Her readily foreseen difficulties resulted from articles she had written for scholarly publications analyzing in provocative and abstruse terms the voting rights law and its implications for race and politics in the United States.

Unlike Baird, who was the victim of an inchoate populist rebellion, Guinier was the target of a calculated assault by the right. On the day after Clinton nominated her, the *Wall Street Journal* ran an op-ed piece by Clint Bolick, the litigation director of the Institute for Justice, a conservative public interest law firm, labeling her "a quota queen." On the basis of two law review articles she had written, Bolick charged that to give an advantage to minorities Guinier would invoke the Voting Rights Act to undermine the principle of one-man, one-vote.[13] Other conservative leaders and organizations soon picked up on the charges as did some Jewish groups, aroused by the incendiary term "quotas."

Meanwhile the White House, having ordered Guinier herself not to respond to the criticism, had almost nothing to say in support of her nomination. Though Guinier was widely respected for her accomplishments as a voting rights attorney, the White House made no attempt to line up prominent leaders either from the world of civil rights or academe to offer testimonials on her behalf. Ralph Neas voiced the resentment of the civil rights leadership.

It was three weeks after the nomination before the White House even sent a letter to the Senate supporting her. They put Lani out there and then abandoned her. And then wouldn't allow her the opportunity to present her case.

The press coverage reflected the course of the controversy—it focused on the attacks on Guinier and offered brief quotes from her controversial articles along with the comments of her supporters. Typical was a story in *USA Today*, two weeks after the appointment was announced. It quoted Bolick as calling Guinier's nomination "the most frontal assault on majority rule in recent memory," and on the other side, offered this sentence: "Defenders say Guinier is a brilliant and inquisitive scholar who is guilty only of 'looking at civil rights issues in new and different ways.'"[14]

Little more than a month after he nominated her, and before the Judiciary Committee held hearings on her nomination, Clinton withdrew her name, saying that her articles, which he claimed to have just then read for the first time, "clearly lend themselves to interpretations that do not represent the views I expressed on civil rights during the campaign."[15]

That decision triggered a wave of indignation from liberals and civil rights groups. Clinton was faulted by liberals who blamed him for not giving Guinier sufficient support to begin with and then preventing her from defending herself before the Senate Judiciary Committee. Some liberal critics also accused the press of irresponsibility in reporting the controversy, and in support of their position now cite a critique in the *Columbia Journalism Review* by Laurel Leff, previously the national legal editor for *American Lawyer*. Leff contended that "too many reporters uncritically accepted Bolick's and other conservatives' depictions of her (Guinier's) views" and "too few reporters made a concerted effort to explain her views on her own terms before offering others' criticisms of them."[16]

But given the complexity of Guinier's writings, the only way the press could put them in perspective was to find scholars who would defend her. And while some in academe contended that the charges against Guinier were unfair and simplistic, they had a hard time themselves explaining in terms clear enough to reassure the public what she did mean. "She has presented some novel tentative ideas on the problem of redistricting," Tulane Law School dean John Kramer told David Savage of the *Los Angeles Times*. "I'm not campaigning for her, but her work is entitled to a fair hearing," said University of Michigan Law School professor Alex Aleinkoff.[17]

Reporters point out that Guinier herself described one controversial article as "academic, very ponderous, very nuanced." "Let me tell you those law review articles which I read are hundreds of pages long and they are impenetrable," said Nina Totenberg of National Public Radio.[18]

The real issue in the controversy, as many reporters realized and some of Guinier's supporters privately acknowledged, was not what Guinier had written, but whether the White House had the political will to face her attackers. "We couldn't have gotten Lani confirmed by arguing about her articles," one civil rights activist told me. "We had to move the argument beyond those damn articles and talk about her qualifications for the job."[19]

But the fight for Guinier had to be led by the White House. It was the White House that could best make the argument that the law review articles were not relevant to her performance in the job for which the president had chosen her and at the same time point to her strengths as a civil rights attorney that presumably had led to her nomination. But Ken Bode among other reporters argued that no such case was made:

> In the Lani Guinier nomination there was no fight. Bill Clinton collapsed before the fight. The defense of Lani Guinier was akin to the campaign of Michael Dukakis. Were we supposed to defend Michael Dukakis when he couldn't defend himself?

Nina Totenberg argued that the decision not to defend Guinier was a calculated effort to cut political losses once the controversy over her nomination had developed:

> Democrats were terrified of the issue of race. They didn't want to have that discussion. Guinier wanted to have it but the Democrats on the Hill didn't want it, and once Clinton realized what was involved he didn't want to have it either. That's a bridge they should have crossed early on and either protected her or not picked her. Those are decisions they didn't make when they should have.

Does this mean that all an interest group has to do is make it hot enough for a presidential nominee and it can force his or her withdrawal? The answer is that it depends on the president and his political objectives. In the cases of Bush and Tower, and Reagan and Bork, each of the Republican presidents decided to wage a fight to the finish, even though the odds were heavily against their nominees winning confirmation. Bush apparently wanted to prove early in his presidency that he was no pushover; Reagan wanted to demonstrate fealty to his conservative supporters who regarded Bork as their champion.

These were both political decisions. Clinton made a different sort of political decision in the Guinier case, even though many believe that had the Senate actually had to vote on Guinier's nomination she might well have prevailed, aided in part by the mounting retrospective indignation at the way the Senate had treated another black woman, Anita Hill. For Clinton, however, the main political imperative was, as Nina Totenberg points out, to avoid a fight over the divisive issue of race. This decision reflected Clinton's position as the leader of a shaky coalition of liberal and centrist Democrats, and also his characteristic desire to seek accommodation and compromise.

Meanwhile, conservative opposition, led by Republican senators, in some cases bolstered by right-wing interest groups, has caused Clinton plenty of trouble with other executive branch appointments, although the media by and large have not treated these controversies as page one or prime-time stories.

Two Clinton nominees in the national security field failed to win confirmation. The nomination of former Colorado state treasurer and former anti-Vietnam war activist Sam Brown as U.S. Ambassador to the Council on Security and Cooperation was blocked by a filibuster led by Colorado senator Hank Brown (no relation). Sam Brown's foes claimed that he lacked experience for the job. Clinton gave up on the fight and dispatched Brown as his representative to the international organization—but without ambassadorial rank.[20] Also rejected because of his record as a dissenter on defense and foreign policy was Clinton's nomination of Morton Halperin to be assistant secretary of defense for peacekeeping and democracy. A former staffer on President Nixon's National Security Council, Halperin was opposed by conservatives because he had defended leakers of secret documents, criticized the CIA, and condemned the U.S. invasions of Grenada and Panama. Clinton withdrew his name, but then appointed him to a staff job on the National Security Council.[21]

A number of other Clinton nominees had to endure substantial criticism before gaining confirmation. Sheldon Hackney, chosen to head the National Endowment for the Humanities, was denounced by conservatives as the "pope of political correctness" because of his handling of campus race issues while he was president of the

University of Pennsylvania.[22] Gay activist Roberta Achtenberg was confirmed as an assistant secretary at the Department of Housing and Urban Development despite Jesse Helms's claim that her past efforts to pressure the Boy Scouts into reversing a ban on homosexual scout-masters meant that she would seek to promote an extremist political agenda in her federal post.[23] Stanford University law professor William B. Gould IV was confirmed by a 58 to 38 vote as the first African-American to chair the National Labor Relations Board after right-wing opponents accused him of antibusiness and prolabor bias.[24]

Jocelyn Elders, the former head of the Arkansas Department of Health, was confirmed by a 65 to 34 vote to be surgeon general after coming under fire for her advocacy of abortion rights and the distribution of condoms.[25] But in office, she continued to provoke criticism from conservatives. And in December 1994, in the most recent example of the deconfirmation process at work, President Clinton fired her for suggesting publicly that masturbation "is part of something that perhaps should be taught in schools."[26]

In another battle that promised more trouble to come, Walter Dellinger, a former Duke University law professor, won confirmation by a 65 to 34 vote as assistant attorney general in charge of the Office of Legal Counsel. Senator Helms led the opposition to Dellinger, who had worked for Helms's opponents in their home state of North Carolina. Helms rallied other Republicans against Dellinger by broadening his personal grudge into a partisan cause, saying a vote against Dellinger was a way of showing the White House that Republicans wanted to be consulted on nominations. Beyond that, Senate aides said that Helms was aware of speculation that Clinton might name Dellinger to a future Supreme Court vacancy, and intended to demonstrate that if Clinton did make that choice he would face a hard battle in the Senate.[27]

Clinton's harsh experience with executive branch nominations might be one reason why he has gone out of his way to avoid a fight over the two Supreme Court nominations he has made. Still another reason for the president's caution is the fact that conservatives are raring for a fight over the Court—in fact they have been gearing up for one since Clinton was elected.

No sooner had the ballots been counted in November 1992 than a fundraising letter sent to 350,000 conservatives signed by Robert Bork asked for money to help fund a new group to monitor court nominees from a conservative standpoint.[28] That organization had been formed a few months earlier, under the overall auspices of Paul Weyrich's Free Congress Foundation and directed by Thomas Jipping, a legal activist who had been involved in mustering support for Bush and Reagan judicial nominees.[29]

Currently, Jipping is still looking for a Supreme Court nominee he can oppose, a reflection of the moderate choices Clinton has made.[30] When Mario Cuomo, his supposed first choice, took himself out of the running for the Supreme Court and Justice Byron White resigned from the Court in spring 1993, Clinton seemed inclined to pick Bruce Babbitt, the former Arizona governor whom he had made secretary of the interior. But then right-wing groups and conservative senators warned that picking Babbitt might lead to a fight. And Clinton settled on a much less controversial choice, Ruth Bader Ginsburg, whom Iowa senator Charles Grassley described as "a Democrat even Republicans can support."[31] Jipping and his cohorts could find little to complain about.

Not that Jipping has been entirely inactive. When Justice Blackmun's resignation in May 1994 gave Clinton another chance to fill a Court vacancy, the president by all accounts leaned toward Babbitt again.[32] Indeed, according to members of Babbitt's own staff, the Interior secretary was persuaded that Clinton had all but made up his mind to pick him.[33]

Meanwhile, though, as it had during the Byron White vacancy, trouble brewed again. Senators Orrin Hatch and Alan Simpson both made plain that they would oppose Babbitt's nomination.[34] And Jipping swung into action. "The game is played differently now than it was two years ago, when the Republicans held the White House," he explained. "But the goal is still the same, to keep liberal activists off the court."[35]

As Clinton appeared close to naming Babbitt to the court in spring 1994, Jipping and his conservative interest group allies in Weyrich's umbrella organization, Coalitions for America, signaled their displeasure, reinforcing opposition from the Senate. "We just made it clear that just as there would be organized opposition (to Babbitt's nomination) in the Senate, that there would also be a lot of opposition from the grass roots perspective," Jipping said.

The White House had other worries, too. Not only would Babbitt's nomination to the Court cause a fight, so would replacing Babbitt. "What they wanted to avoid was a full-scale debate over

Federal lands policy in the Senate, in an election year," said one administration official.[36] If that happened the administration would be caught between the fires of Republican conservatives who opposed administration lands policies as too liberal and the environmental interest groups who complained they were not liberal enough.

8

Summary and Conclusions

The Interest Groups

Looking back at the conservative opposition to Clinton's middle level appointments during his first two years, Ralph Neas contended that the assault from the right represented a change in "the rules of engagement" for confirmation fights. In the past, Neas argued, these have been limited mainly to the appointment of judges who, he points out, serve for life and are supposedly independent, while executive branch nominees serve at the pleasure of the president and are subject to congressional oversight.

This argument overstates the case, though not by much. As Neas acknowledges, his own organization led the fight against three important executive branch nominations during the Reagan-Bush years—Ed Meese, to be attorney general; William Bradford Reynolds, to be associate attorney general; and William Lucas, whom Bush chose to head the civil rights division. He claims that there were special circumstances in each case and points out that only three such challenges occurred during the twelve Republican White House years.

Neas's argument in part reflects the fact that some interest group leaders still feel uncomfortable about their role in the nominating process because it makes them vulnerable to criticism that they are interfering with the president and obstructing the government. Some conservatives, notably Paul Weyrich, attempt to draw the same line that Neas does between judicial and executive branch appointments. Weyrich said:

One should more readily oppose a lifetime nominee to the Court than a presidential appointee to one of the departments. As bad as Jocelyn Elders is in my view she does represent Clinton. I did not oppose her. He is entitled to an appointment like that by virtue of having won the election.

But this assertion overlooks the fact that it was Weyrich who sparked the battle against John Tower, an executive branch nomination made by a president of his own party. And as noted previously, a number of middle-level executive branch nominations made by Ford, Carter, and Reagan had come under attack for a variety of reasons from right and left. Moreover, Mark Gitenstein recalls that during the Reagan presidency, when he was chief counsel to the Senate Judiciary Committee, "Groups on the left lobbied the hell out of us" to oppose executive branch nominees they regarded as hostile to civil rights.

The truth is that an escalation has been taking place even though it is has been developing for a longer period than Neas contends. And though it has not happened overnight, the judicial-executive line of demarcation has been losing much of its meaning as contentiousness increases across the board of the appointment process. In fact, Clint Bolick argues that executive branch nominees should be subject to closer scrutiny than judges:

> Judicial nominees should not be asked how they would rule on specific cases. But executive branch nominees should be asked how they would enforce the laws. In that degree the questions can be more probing. That is why we thought Guinier's writings were so relevant. They related to laws that she would be enforcing.[1]

In sum, though not all interest groups like to admit it, more of them seem to be deciding whether to oppose a nomination simply on the basis of whether they have a reasonable chance to prevail. In a world in which presidential prestige is declining, political parties are eroding, and the electorate is fragmenting, the notion that a president has as a right to appoint whom he pleases is fast losing favor. Instead, presidential appointments increasingly are viewed as just another political trophy and the confirmation process just another political battle ground. "The president makes political appointments to pursue political objectives," argued American Conservative Union chairman David Keene, "and his political objectives are legitimate fodder to argue about."

This trend seemed likely to continue during the Clinton presidency even before the votes were counted in the 1994 congressional elections, and the results of those elections obviously make the future even more difficult for the president. With the Senate in Republican hands, right-wing interest groups will be even more emboldened to challenge any attempt on his part which seems to them as an attempt to undo the gains conservatives made during the Reagan-Bush era, which is why they challenged so many executive branch nominees during the first half of his first term.

"Clinton has appointed more ideologues to the executive branch than to the judicial branch," Clint Bolick of the Institute for Justice told me. "This reflects his own priorities."

"We opposed both the nominations of Sam Brown and Mort Halperin because we felt that the public was being asked to ratify their view of society," said David Keene, "and they made no change in terms of rhetoric or any other way from their activities in the 1960s."

Meanwhile, Clinton will still be under pressure from liberals, many of whom have so far been disappointed by some aspects of his performance, to make the sort of appointments which are likely to invite resistance from the right. "I had the impression that Clinton wanted to appoint Babbitt, but that folks in the White House looked at it and said he won't get 100 votes but he'll get more than 80 votes," said Jim Maddy, head of the League of Conservation Voters.

> And somehow to my surprise that was deemed to be too controversial, that it would take too much attention away from something else. And then when they said to themselves, "Who would we get at Interior?," they said, "We've got environmentalists irritated with us, we've got the commodity interests up in arms. Selecting an interior secretary in this atmosphere will be too contentious." Both sides are genuinely irritated. The commodity interests feel like they lost the election, and so they are fighting with everything they've got. And they are not surprised. But we feel like we won and so we are surprised to be so disappointed in the results.[2]

Even though the midterm elections cost the Democrats control of Congress, liberals will still expect Clinton to make the most of the prestige and authority of the presidency in the appointment process.

Looking back at the great battles of the past, interest groups on each side of the spectrum blame the other side for the intensifying contentiousness. Said Nan Aron, head of the Alliance for Justice, which has been in the forefront of the fight over court nominations:

> Confirmations are contentious because Ronald Reagan and George Bush set out to change the face of the judiciary. Reagan wanted to put ideologues on the federal bench because he couldn't dismantle legal services, couldn't blunt reenactment of voting rights, so he turned to the Federal courts.[3]

On the right, Thomas Jipping of the Judicial Monitoring Project attributes the contentiousness over nominations to the increasing tendency of federal courts to take on political issues "and sticking their hands in." Jipping added:

> If the courts were involved in a narrower range of issues the way they should be you wouldn't have a politically contentious selection process. One way to depoliticize judicial selection is to dejudicialize a lot of political issues.

In a sense they are both right—which helps explain the outlook for continued contentiousness on judicial appointments. Reagan and Bush did appoint a good many conservative judges to stem the tide of legal activism, and they still remain in control of most of the seats in the appellate courts.[4] Their continued presence will spur pressure from liberals like Nan Aron to get Clinton to replace them with jurists as far to the left as the Reagan-Bush appointees are to the right. Meanwhile the increasing involvement of the federal judiciary in new areas that Jipping finds objectionable will likely continue, in part because of the 1994 crime bill, which legal experts predict will flood the federal courts with cases touching on such sensitive issues as gun control and domestic violence that once the states dealt with exclusively.

THE MEDIA

As this paper demonstrates, the role of the media in the presidential appointment process is significant but almost always secondary. The exact nature of media involvement varies with circumstances. In the

Clarence Thomas furor, as in the Haynsworth and Carswell controversies, press disclosures contributed to the contentiousness. In the
Bork case, the media served mainly as Stephen Hess put it, as "a conveyor belt" for arguments made by both sides. In other recent controversies involving lower level appointments, the media role was
incidental.

Most journalists reject the idea that the press has a defining role
in the appointment process. "My instinct is that confirmation fights
are not primarily a press phenomenon," said the chief political writ-
er at the *Washington Post*, David Broder. "We have had a number of
spirited battles that simply resulted from divided government."[5]

And most interest group activists view the press as a flawed but useful neutral instrument. "The press tends to focus on sexy and irrelevant things," said conservative activist Jipping, expressing a sentiment
echoed by his liberal counterparts. "But it's very important in getting
information across. It's sort of like a loaded gun, you can use it for
good or bad purposes."

Criticisms of the press's role in the confirmation conflicts are much
the same as the criticism of press coverage of politics and government
and other elements of society. One common charge is typified by the
comment of Paul Weaver, author of *News and the Culture of Lying*:

> Modern news coverage isn't simply a report of what hap-
> pened yesterday. It's a story with characters, action, plot,
> point of view, dramatic disclosure. And in particular it's
> often a story about crisis and emergency response.[6]

Similarly, Ralph Neas of the Leadership Conference, while generally approving of press coverage, complains:

> The only time we can get adequate press coverage of issue is
> when there is a confrontation or adversary relationship. The
> thing I most consistently have a problem with is the inabili-
> ty of the press to focus on substantive issues, really getting
> into subject matter rather than focusing almost exclusively
> on process and politics.

It could be argued, however, that when the press does pay more
attention to substance than its critics acknowledge, such stories often
are overlooked or forgotten because they do not get the attention
paid to other more dramatic stories, nor do they have that much

impact. In defense of the press, Ken Bode says: "When people bash the press they always forget that there were hundreds of stories written about Clarence Thomas's background his values and his record and so forth until Anita Hill came along."

Moreover, the press's sometimes personalized approach to the appointment process, while derided by some critics, if done well, can contribute to public understanding of the nominee and how he or she will perform if confirmed. Says Bode:

> The first thing people want to know when they hear the name Stephen Breyer is not that he made his career in regulation law. They know they've got this guy on the Court for the rest of his life. They want to know who is this guy, how did he get where he is and why has he been nominated. And we get one chance to tell the story about a Supreme Court nominee and that's before he's nominated.

As the critics complain, investigative journalism that has been given more emphasis from an increasingly aggressive and skeptical press sometimes leads to excess. But such probing also sometimes produces significant and illuminating revelations, as with the disclosure that some members of the Senate Judiciary Committee had been informed of Anita Hill's sexual harassment charges against Clarence Thomas. "That's the quintessence of what we are supposed to do," said Nina Totenberg, who played a role in breaking the story. She added:

> The Judiciary Committee didn't do its job. They never listened to her complaints, never talked to her in any serious manner, never went out and investigated in a way that could have made it a quiet and reasonable and thorough investigation. So what happened? The watchdog is supposed to find out when they don't do their jobs, and that's what we did. I always thought that at least half that story had to do with the Judiciary Committee and not Clarence Thomas.

At any rate, journalistic muckraking is a long and arguably honorable American tradition going much further back than Watergate or Iran-Contra. And while media technology has changed and competitiveness has intensified with the emergence of new electronic outlets for information, print reporters reject the notion that these trends have made them more eager or less meticulous about digging up negative information about a nominee. Gaylord Shaw, Washington Bureau chief of *Newsday* which led the way in reporting Judge Breyer's ties to a Lloyds of London insurance syndicate, recalls the fight over Fortas's nomination to be chief justice in 1968. "There was the same degree of interest then as there was in Clarence Thomas or in Breyer," he said.[7] As for television, Shaw says:

> So much of the media just focus on surface. Our role is to go after stories that won't show up of their own accord. I don't consider *Newsday* in competition with CNN or Hard Copy or anybody else. Did CNN break any of the stuff on Breyer and Lloyds of London?

Simply by its existence, television has enlarged the impact of the fruits of investigative journalism on the appointment process.[8] "Television magnifies everything," says Common Cause's Fred Wertheimer:

> You put something negative in print you read it and go on to something else. You put it on television and it goes on in your head like a flashing bulb. Television is emotion not thought process.

Interest group leaders have learned to live with the phenomenon of television. As Ralph Neas acknowledges: "We spend a lot of time making sure that when you have only 30 seconds (on television) you convey what you want to convey, not what the reporter wants to convey." But there is no convincing evidence that television, or the other technological advances in the media in recent years, have shaped fundamental strategy by interest groups such as whether or not to undertake a confirmation fight. Interest group leaders say they have their own independent criteria and priorities that determine such decisions.

How much influence do interest groups have on the media? The answer depends on the effectiveness of the interest groups against which they are competing and the professionalism of the individual reporters with whom they deal. "They have figured out that information is a lever into the debate," said Ken Bode:

When I covered Stephen Breyer for public television, the best information we had was provided not by the White House but all these various interest groups including Weyrich and Neas. It was the most detailed, and it was the most thorough. We understood it to have a point of view. The take that Neas would have was not necessarily the case Weyrich would have. The point is they had interesting things to say and it was up to us to decide where we would fit it in. I read their stuff carefully. And I always remembered where it came from.

"I'm an old-school reporter," said Bill Eaton. "I think you have to take the interest group allegations with a lot of salt. But if they stand up you have to use them."

The truth is that a major nomination now offers so much potential as a story that newspapers nowadays don't need much pressure from interest groups to investigate. Noting that Ralph Nader had seized upon the Breyer's Lloyds of London ties to raise the conflict of interest issue, Gaylord Shaw said:

We did work on Breyer and Lloyds of London before the Nader people even said boo on it. We looked at the financial disclosure statement filed by federal judges. Long before the Nader people said anything, we already had the stuff and were working on it. These sources weren't supplied to us. We were hiring correspondents in London who were knowledgeable on Lloyds of London. We knew the Nader people were interested but they weren't the driving force. We take anything and everything people give us in the way of leads. We think we have got a pretty good record of developing this stuff on our own. It would be good if people handed us stuff that we could trust and run. But we don't live in that kind of world. And I like it better the way it is.

CONSEQUENCES

To those who believe that the purpose of the appointment process is simply to expeditiously ratify presidential choices for high office, the surge in contentiousness is certainly alarming. To others, the recent decline in presidential prestige and the mounting public cynicism toward all governmental institutions suggests that a different and broader view of the process should be adopted. After all, the phrase "presidential appointment process" is in itself a misnomer, at least according to the Constitution. Article II, Section II, Clause II states that the president "shall nominate, and by and with the Advice and Consent of the Senate shall appoint Ambassadors, other public Ministers and Consuls, Judges of the Supreme Court and all other officers of the United States whose appointments are not otherwise provided for."[9]

It is true, as this paper points out, that for most of our history this senatorial authority was more often honored in the breach. It is also true that during these years presidents did not always cover themselves with glory by their appointments. The use of ambassadorships to reward rich contributors by nearly all our chief executives is only one way in which this prerogative has been abused. In view of the past and present circumstances, I think contentiousness over presidential nominations is not always to be condemned or avoided. Rather each case should be judged on its own merits. At any rate, that seems to be what is happening. What the ultimate impact of this trend on presidents and the presidency will be, no one can foretell. To be sure, even some interest group leaders who have been active in opposing nominations profess to be concerned about the alleged bad effects of contentiousness. "It does keep really good people out at the top level. And it makes presidents and personnel shops shy away from people who are controversial," said David Keene.

"I think you have to do this (oppose nominations) very sparingly," said Paul Weyrich, adding:

> My thinking has advanced to the point that I now believe we would be better off if we had a parliamentary system. There you would have a clear majority in the legislature. You could put forth who you wanted and the people could see where you wanted to go. The problem now is it gets all fuzzed up.

But others, on both the left and right, disagree. Clint Bolick thinks that confrontations over presidential nominations are worth having for their own sake: "I think that a good confirmation battle is adrenaline for America's democratic soul." His explanation, while somewhat self-serving, nevertheless reflects the view of many on the other side of the ideological fence, and on the losing side of the Lani Guinier controversy. Bolick said:

Part of the problem with this administration is this president doesn't seem to have courage of his convictions. I don't think there's anything wrong with nominating a controversial nominee, but make it an honest and full and fair debate over underlying ideas. What would happen if a president said, "Yes this nominee does have controversial ideas, but I happen to agree with them"?

Moreover, just as the interest groups have a right to oppose presidential nominations, the president has the right, and in some cases an obligation, not to yield to their pressure, and stands a chance to benefit from such a stance. "Sometimes a good fight is a good thing for a president, particularly when its something as important as a Supreme Court nomination," said Ralph Neas.

This point is particularly relevant in view of the new Republican majority now ruling the Senate. "The pressure on President Clinton to be too accomodating (in making appointments) has increased substantially since the election," the *Washington Post* cautioned in an editorial the week after the midterm vote:

> The President has not only the power but the responsibility to choose judges and high officials. . . . It would be a mistake for the president to yield preemptively instead of working with responsible members of Congress in support of his own nominees.[10]

By standing firm, Clinton can serve not only his own political interest but also benefit the ailing political process. Said Terry Eastland of *Forbes Media Critic* about the contentious appointment process:

> I don't know how to put this genie back into the bottle, and anyhow this may not be the worst thing in the world. When you get into a substantive confirmation fight, that's American democracy at work. It may be the only time you can get people to focus on what their government does.

NOTES

1

1. Gwen Ifil, "Babbitt Waits as Clinton Ponders Successor," *New York Times*, May 12, 1994, p. A16.

2. "Breyer's Liberal, Conservative Mix Seems to Assure Confirmation," *Congressional Quarterly Weekly Report*, May 21, 1994, p. 1305.

3. Linda Greenhouse, "A Cloud on the Breyer Nomination," *New York Times*, July 26, 1994, p. A24.

4. Author's interview, July 12, 1994

5. Author's interview, August 3, 1994.

6. "A Cloud on the Breyer Nomination," *New York Times*, July 26, 1994, p. A20.

7. Linda Greenhouse, "Breyer Wins Confirmation," *New York Times*, July 30, 1994, p. A19.

8. Art Pine, "Inman Was Unprepared for Heat," *Los Angeles Times*, January 20, 1994, p. A20.

9. Steven A. Holmes, "Blacks Relent on Crime Bill," *New York Times*, June 13, 1994, p. A1.

10. Robert Shogan, "Clinton Risks Image as Reed in the Wind," *Los Angeles Times*, June 13, 1994, p. A1.

11. David G. Savage, "Smooth Sailing Forecast for Breyer," *Los Angeles Times*, July 12, 1994, p. A12.

12. Author's interview, July 13, 1994.

13. Ethan Bronner, *Battle for Justice* (New York: W. W. Norton, 1989), p. 347.

14. Author's interview, August 2, 1994. See also, "Some Comments Regarding Changing Standards for Executive Branch Nominations," Leadership Conference on Civil Rights press release, Washington, D.C., February 8, 1994.

15. Lloyd Cutler, "To Form A Government," *Foreign Affairs* (Fall 1980): 42.

162   OBSTACLE COURSE

16. Morris Janowitz, *The Last Half Century* (Chicago: University of Chicago Press, 1978), pp. 15–26.

17. Gallup poll, August 16, 1981, in Robert Shogan, *None of the Above* (New York: New American Library, 1983), p. 9.

18. Tom Rosenstiel, *The Beat Goes On* (New York: The Twentieth Century Fund Press, 1994), p. 30.

19. Tom Wicker, "What's the Uproar About," *New York Times,* July 25, 1994, p. A25.

20. Everett Carll Ladd, "Down on Politics," *Christian Science Monitor,* October 21, 1994, p. 15.

21. G. Calvin Mackenzie, memorandum to Jon Shure, September 9, 1994.

22. Author's interview, September 28, 1994.

23. Author's interview, September 27, 1994.

24. Mackenzie, op. cit.

25. Author's interview, August 9, 1994.

26. Rosenstiel, *The Beat Goes On*, p. 30.

27. Jeff Gerth, "Quiet Handling of a Nominee's S. & L. Tenure," *New York Times,* July 22, 1994, p. A1.

28. Guy Gugliotta, "Regarding Henry," *Washington Post,* October 12, 1994.

29. Sanford J. Ungar, *The Papers and the Papers* (New York: Dutton Books, 1972), pp. 168–69.

30. Author's interview, September 26, 1994. See also Charles O. Jones, *The Presidency in a Separated System* (Washington, D.C.: The Brookings Institution, 1994).

31. The two exceptions to this rule during that period was the one-term Carter presidency from 1977 to 1981, and the Republican majority in the Senate from 1981 through 1987.

32. Author's interview, August 2, 1994.

33. Author's interview, August 9, 1994.

34. Benjamin Ginsberg and Martin Shefter, *Politics by Other Means* (New York: Basic Books, 1990), p. 1.

35. Author's interview, August 1, 1994.

36. Author's interview, August 7, 1994.

2

1. Confirmation proceedings tended to be more acrimonious in the nineteenth century, when the Senate rejected one out of three nominees to the Supreme Court. Mark Silverstein attributes this to the strong influence of state party organizations on the Senate, whose

members were then appointed by state legislatures, and who tended to view court appointees as another prize of the spoils system and were often unwilling to defer to presidents, even on Supreme Court appointments, which they viewed simply as an elevated form of patronage. See Mark Silverstein, *Judicious Choices: The New Politics of Supreme Court Confirmations* (New York: W. W. Norton, 1994), p. 3.

2. Stephen L. Carter, *The Confirmation Mess* (New York: Basic Books, 1994).

3. William F. Swindler, *Court and Constitution in the 20th Century: The New Legality 1932–1968* (New York: Bobbs-Merrill, 1970), pp. 82–87.

4. Author's interview with Professor Philip B. Kurland, University of Chicago, June 12, 1993.

5,. *New York Times*, January 13, 1939; Dean Acheson, *Morning and Noon* (New York: Houghton Mifflin, 1965), p. 209.

6. Swindler, *Court and Constitution in the 20th Century*, p. 225.

7. Ibid.

8. Ibid., p. 226.

9. Ibid., p. 332.

10. Carter, *The Confrontation Mess*, p. 5.

11. Ibid., p. 6.

12. Author's interview, October 7, 1994.

3

1. James F. Simon, *In His Own Image* (New York: McKay, 1973), p. 21.

2. Ronald Steel, *Walter Lippmann and the American Century* (New York: Vintage Books, 1981), p. 558.

3. Texts of Nixon campaign speeches, October 3, 1968 and October 21, 1968. Also Richard M. Nixon, *Nixon on the Issues* (Nixon-Agnew Campaign Committee, New York, 1968).

4. Lewis Chester, et. al, *An American Melodrama* (New York: Viking Penguin, 1969), pp. 461–63.

5. Robert Shogan, *A Question of Judgment* (New York: Bobbs Merrill, 1972), pp. 143–60.

6. Mark Silverstein, *Judicious Choices: The New Politics of Supreme Court Confirmations* (New York: Norton, 1994), p. 129.

7. Shogan, *A Question of Judgment*, pp. 160–84.

8. Ibid., pp. 262–67.

9. Philip Kurland, "The Disciplining of Justice Fortas," *Chicago Sun Times*, April 23, 1972, p. 15.

10. Shogan, *A Question of Judgment*, pp. 271–72.
11. Richard Harris, *Decision* (New York: Dutton, 1971), p. 105.
12. Ibid., p. 94.
13. Ibid., p. 55.
14. Ibid., p. 106.
15. Ibid., p. 272.
16. Ibid., p. 209.
17. Shogan, *A Question of Judgment*, p. 274.

4

1. Gerald R. Ford, *A Time to Heal* (New York: Harper & Row, 1979), pp. 207, 209, 223–24.
2. *Congressional Quarterly Almanac 1974* (Washington, D.C.: Congressional Quarterly, Inc., 1974), p. 953.
3. Ibid.
4. *Congressional Quarterly Almanac 1975* (Washington, D.C.: Congressional Quarterly, Inc., 1975), p. 936.
5. *Congressional Quarterly Almanac 1975* (Washington, D.C.: Congressional Quarterly, Inc., 1975), p. 967.
6. John Robert Greene, *The Limits of Power* (Bloomington: Indiana University Press, 1992), p. 229.
7. Robert Shogan, *Promises to Keep* (New York: Crowell, 1977), pp. 91–92.
8. Ibid., p. 218.
9. Charles O. Jones, *The Trusteeship Presidency* (Baton Rouge: Louisiana State University Press, 1988), pp. 150–53.

5

1. Author's interview, July 6, 1994.
2. Lou Cannon, *Ronald Reagan: The Role of a Lifetime* (New York: Simon & Schuster, 1991), p. 798.
3. *Congressional Quarterly Almanac 1981*, (Washington, D.C.: Congressional Quarterly, Inc., 1981), p. 18A.
4. *Congressional Quarterly Almanac 1982*, pp. 412, 21A.
5. *Congressional Quarterly Almanac 1982*, p. 21A.
6. *Congressional Quarterly Almanac 1982*, p. 419.
7. Leadership Conference on Civil Rights press release, March 5, 1984.
8. Author's interview, August 3, 1994.
9. Leadership Conference press release, June 5, 1985.

10. *Congressional Quarterly Almanac 1985*, p. 237.

11. Author's interview, August 2, 1994.

12. Ethan Bronner, "Passing Judgment," *Boston Globe Magazine*, August 27, 1989, p. 18.

13. James Warren, "Bork Fight Paved Way for Thomas Ads," *Chicago Tribune*, September 6, 1991, p. 1.

14. Ethan Bonner, *Battle for Justice* (New York: W. W. Norton, 1989), pp. 98–99.

15. Bonner, "Passing Judgment."

16. Bonner, *Battle for Justice*, p. 160.

17. Ibid., p. 308.

18. Warren, "Bork Fight Paved Way for Thomas Ads."

19. Bonner, *Battle for Justice*, p. 351.

6

1. *Congressional Quarterly Almanac 1989* (Washington, D.C.: Congressional Quarterly, Inc., 1989), p. 403.

2. *Public Papers of the Presidents: George Bush, 1989,* Book I (Washington, D.C.: Government Printing Office, 1990), pp. 16, 65.

3. Author's interview, February 14, 1989.

4. Timothy M. Phelps and Helen Winternitz, *Capitol Games* (New York: Harper Collins, 1993), p. 15.

5. David Savage, *Turning Right* (New York: John Wiley & Sons, 1992), p. 435; Phelps and Winternitz, *Capitol Games*, p. 141.

6. Savage, *Turning Right*, p. 431.

7. Ibid.

8. Phelps and Winternitz, *Capitol Games*, p. 13.

9. Ibid., pp. 132–34.

10. James Warren, "Bork Fight Paved Way for Thomas Ads," *Chicago Tribune*, September 6, 1991, p. 1.

11. Phelps and Winternitz, *Capitol Games*, p. 224.

12. Ibid., p. 227.

13. Ibid., p. 232.

14. Phelps and Winternitz, *Capitol Games*, p. 419.

7

1. Author's interview, June 28, 1994.

2. Author's interview with confidential source, December 16, 1992.

3. *New York Times*, December 22, 1992, p. A1.

4. *New York Times*, December 22, 1992, pp. A16, A17.

5. Stuart Taylor, "Inside the Whirlwind," *The American Lawyer*, March 1993. Except as otherwise indicated, this article is the main source for the recounting of the Baird controversy.

6. *New York Times*, January 14, 1993, p. A1.

7. *New York Times*, January 15, 1993, p. A26; *Washington Post*, January 15, 1993, p. A24.

8. Tom Rosenstiel, *Strange Bedfellows* (New York: Hyperion Press, 1994), pp. 164–71.

9. Author's interview, July 11, 1994.

10. Elizabeth Shogren, "Calls Against Baird Flooding Talk Shows," *Los Angeles Times*, January 22, 1993, p. A26.

11. Robert Reinhold, "An Angry Public . . . Outcry Becomes Uproar," *New York Times*, January 23, 1993, Section 1, p. 9.

12. David Broder, "A Lot to Learn from the Baird Affair, *Washington Post*, January 26, 1993, p. A17.

13. Clint Bolick, "Clinton's Quota Queens," *Wall Street Journal*, April 30, 1993.

14. Tony Mauro, "Two Clinton Nominees Face Tough Sledding," *USA Today*, May 14, 1993, p. A6.

15. David Savage, "Guinier's Articles Viewed as Largely Theoretical," *Los Angeles Times*, June 5, 1993, p. A14.

16. Laurel Leff, "From Legal Scholar to Quota Queen," *Columbia Journalism Review*, September-October 1993, p. 36.

17. David G. Savage, "Paper Trail Could Block Nominee for Justice Post," *Los Angeles Times*, Saturday, May 22, 1993, p. A1.

18. Author's interview, July 12, 1994.

19. Author's interview with confidential source, July 19, 1994.

20. Jim Mann and Michael Ross,"Washington Insight," *Los Angeles Times*, May 30, 1994, p. A5; John Brinkley, "'Non-Ambassador' Brown to Represent U.S.," *Rocky Mountain News*, June 10, 1994, p. A20.

21. Steve Komarow, "Defense Post in Controversy," *USA Today*, November 17, 1993, p. A4; *Washington Times*, June 9, 1994, p. A12.

22. Michael Ross, "Sheldon Hackney Picked," *Los Angeles Times*, June 26, 1993, p.A2.

23. Michael Ross, "Gay Activist OKd," *Los Angeles Times*, May 25, 1993, p. A3.

24. Robert L. Jackson, "Stanford Professor Sworn In," *Los Angeles Times*, March 9, 1994, p. A21.

25. Marlene Cimons, "Senate Confirms Elders," *Los Angeles Times*, September 8, 1993, p. Al.

26. Ruth Marcus, "President Clinton Fires Elders," *Washington Post*, December 19, 1994, p. 1A.

27. Stephen Laboton, "Helms Filibusters against a Nominee," *New York Times*, October 8, 1993. p. A20.

28. Neil A. Lewis, "Conservative Set for Fight," *New York Times*, November 13, 1992, p. A16.

29. W. John Moore, "Judges on the Left! Hold That Line," *National Journal*, May 22, 1993, p. 1246.

30. Clinton has not had many problems with his lower court nominees, either. In August 1994, the *Washington Post* noted that only two of Clinton's nineteen appointees to the Federal Court of Appeals have had to undergo individual hearings before the Judiciary Committee. "With little exception Clinton's nominations have received scant scrutiny by Senators and glided through the process." (Joan Biskupic, "Senate to Grill Judicial Nominee," *Washington Post*, August 3, 1994.)

31. "Clinton Closes In on a Nominee," *Congressional Quarterly Weekly Report*, June 12, 1993, p. 1482.

32. Ann Devroy, "Boston Judge Breyer Nominated to High Court," *Washington Post*, May 14, 1994, p. Al.

33. Author's interview with confidential source, May 15, 1994.

34. Gwen Ifil, "Babbitt Waits as Clinton Ponders Successor," *New York Times*, May 12, 1994, p. A16.

35. Author's interview, July 12, 1994.

36. Author's interview with confidential source, May 15, 1994.

8

1. Author's interview, August 4, 1994.

2. Author's interview, August 8, 1994.

3. Author's interview, July 12, 1994.

4. Stephen Labaton, "President's Judicial Appointments Diverse," *New York Times*, October 17, 1994, p. A13.

5. Author's interview, June 28, 1994.

6. Paul H. Weaver, "Selling the Story," *New York Times*, July 29, 1994, p. A27.

7. Author's interview, August 10, 1994.

8. This did not happen in the case of *Newsday's* coverage of Breyer, apparently because the allegations were too complex and technical to cover in sixty seconds or so of television time.

9. Taylor W. O'Hearn, *The Constitution of the United States With Explanations,* (Shreveport, La.: A.P.H. Publishers, 1986), p. 34.

10. "The President's Nominees," *Washington Post,* November 18, 1994, p. A24.

APPENDIXES

Appendix 1

THE WHITE HOUSE
WASHINGTON

PERSONAL DATA STATEMENT QUESTIONNAIRE

FROM: OFFICE OF COUNSEL TO THE PRESIDENT

As part of the clearance procedures for your prospective position, please answer all of the following questions (please do not respond "not applicable" or "N/A" If your response is "no" or "none"). In responding to the questions, please supply any information regarding your spouse or relatives that you deem to be relevant. Your responses to this questionnaire, which is not subject to public disclosure, are confidential.

You can type your responses in memorandum form on a separate sheet of paper with each answer corresponding to the number of the question. You do not need to retype the questions, but please sign and date the response.

Because your appointment cannot be finalized until all necessary reviews have been completed, and because our review begins with receipt of your paperwork, please supply this information within **24 hours** to **Clifford J. Mauton** in this office. (**Old Executive Office Building, Room 136, Washington, D.C. 20500; fax number: (202) 456-2146**).

If you have any questions or need assistance in responding to this questionnaire, please do not hesitate to contact this office at 202-456-6229. Thank you for your cooperation.

Personal and Family Background

1. Please list your full name; home address and telephone number; office address and telephone number; date and place of birth; citizenship; and social security number.

2. Please identify your current marital status; spouse's name, citizenship, occupation, and current employer; and the names and ages of your children.

3.   Do you have any medical conditions that could interfere with your ability to
fulfill your duties? Please explain.

Professional and Educational Background

4.   Please list each high school, college, and graduate school you attended; the dates of your attendance; and degrees awarded.

5.   Please furnish a copy of your resume and a brief biographical statement.

6.   Please chronologically list activities, other than those listed on your resume, from which you have derived earned income (e.g., self-employment, consulting activities, writing, speaking, royalties, and honoraria) since age 21.

7.   Please list each book, article, column or publication you have authored, individually or with others.

8.   Identify each instance in which you have testified before Congress in a non-governmental capacity and specify the subject matter of each testimony.

9.   Please list all corporations, partnerships, trusts, or other business entities with which you have ever been affiliated as an officer, director, trustee, partner, or holder of a significant equity or financial interest (i.e., any ownership interest of more than 5%), or whose decisions you had the ability to influence. Please identify the entity, your relationship to the entity, and dates of service and/or affiliation.

10.   Please provide the names of all corporations, firms, partnerships, trusts, or other business enterprises, and all non-profit organizations and other institutions with which you are now, or during the past five years have been, affiliated as an advisor, attorney or consultant. It is only necessary to provide the names of major clients and any client matter in which you and your firm are involved that might present a potential conflict of interest with your proposed assignment. Please include dates of service.

11. With regard to each of the entities identified in the preceding question, please identify your relationship or duty with regard to each. Please include dates of service.

12. Other than the entities identified in question number 10 above, please provide the names of any organizations with which you were associated which might present a potential conflict of interest with your proposed assignment. For each entity you identified in your response to this question please provide your relationship or duty with regard to each. Please include dates of service.

13. Please describe any contractual or informal arrangement you may have made with any person or any business enterprise in regard to future employment or termination payments or financial benefits that will be provided you if you enter government employment.

14. If you are a member of any licensed profession or occupation (such as lawyer, doctor, accountant, insurance or real estate broker, etc.), please specify: the present status of each license; and whether any such license has ever been withdrawn, suspended, or revoked, and the reason therefor.

15. Do you have a significant interest in any relationship with the government through contracts, consulting services, grants, loans or guarantees? If yes, please provide details.

16. Does your spouse or any family member or business in which you, your spouse or any family members have a significant interest have any relationship with the federal government through contracts, consulting services, grants, loans or guarantees? If yes, please provide details.

17. If you have performed any work for and/or received any payments from any foreign government, business, or individual in the past 10 years, please describe the circumstances, and identify the source, and dates of services and/or payments.

18. Please list any registration as an agent for a foreign principal, or any exemption from such registration. Please provide the status of any and all such registrations and/or exemptions (i.e., whether active and whether personally registered).

19. Have you ever registered as a lobbyist or other legislative agent to influence federal or state legislation or administrative acts? If yes, please supply details including the status of each registration.

Tax and Financial Information

20. As of the date of this questionnaire, please list all assets with a fair market value in excess of $1,000 for you and your spouse and provide a good faith estimate of value.

21. As of the date of this questionnaire, please list all liabilities in excess of $10,000 for you and your spouse. Please list the name and address of the creditor, the amount owed to the nearest thousand dollar, a brief description of the nature of the obligation, the interest rate (if any), the date on which due, and the present status (i.e., is the obligation current or past due).

22. Please describe all real estate held in your name or in your spouse's name during the last six years. Please include real estate held in combination with others, held in trust, held by a nominee, or held by or through any other third person or title-holding entity. Please also include dates held.

23. Have you and your spouse filed all federal, state and local income tax returns?

24. Have you or your spouse ever filed a late income tax return without a valid extension? If so, describe the circumstances and the resolution of the matter.

25. Have you or your spouse ever paid any tax penalties? If so, describe the circumstances and the resolution of the matter.

26. Has a tax lien or other collection procedure ever been instituted against you or your spouse by federal, state or local authorities? If so, describe the circumstances and the resolution of the matter.

Domestic Help Issue

27. Do you presently have or have you in the past had domestic help? (i.e., a housekeeper, babysitter, nanny, or gardener) If yes, please indicate years of service for each individual and also give a brief description of the services rendered.

Public and Organizational Activities

28. Please list current and past political party affiliations.

29. Have you ever run for public office? If yes, does your campaign have any outstanding campaign debt? If so, are you personally liable? Please also provide complete information as to amount of debt and creditors.

30. Please list each membership you have had with any civic, social, charitable, educational, professional, fraternal, benevolent or religious organization, private club, or other membership organization (including any tax-exempt organization) during the past 10 years. Please include dates of membership and any positions you may have had with the organization.

31. Have you or your spouse at any time belonged to any membership organization, including but not limited to those described in the preceding paragraph, that as a matter of policy or practice denied or restricted affiliation (as a matter of either policy or practice) based on race, sex, ethnic background, religious or sexual preference?

Legal and Administrative Proceedings and Filings

32. Please list any lawsuits you have brought as a plaintiff or which were brought against you as a defendant or third party. Include in this response any contested divorce proceedings or other domestic relations matters.

33. Please list and describe any administrative agency proceeding in which you have been involved as a party.

34. Please list any bankruptcy proceeding in which you or your spouse have been involved as a debtor.

35. Have you or your spouse ever been investigated by any federal, state, military or local law enforcement agency? If so, please identify each such instance and supply details, including: date; place; law enforcement agency; and court.

36. Have you or your spouse ever been arrested for or charged with, or convicted of violating any federal, state or local law, regulation or ordinance (excluding traffic offenses for which the fine was less than $100)? If so, please identify each such instance and supply details, including: date; place; law enforcement agency; and court.

37. Have you or your spouse ever been accused of or found guilty of any violations of government or agency procedure (specifically including security violations and/or any application, or appeal process)?

38. Please list any complaint ever made against you or by any administrative agency, professional association or organization, or federal, state or local ethics agency, committee, or official.

39. Please list any and all judgments rendered against you including the date, amount, the name of the case and subject matter of the case, and the date of satisfaction. Please include obligations of child support and alimony and provide the status of each judgement and/or obligation.

40. With regard to each obligation of child support and/or alimony, please state the following: Have any payments been made late or have there been any lapses in payment? Have any motions or court actions for modification of child support or alimony been filed or instituted? Have any actions or motions to compel payment or initiate collection of late payments and/or past due amounts been filed or threatened? Have any writs of garnishment been issued? If your response was yes to any of the above questions, please provide details.

Miscellaneous

41. Have you ever had any association with any person, group or business venture that could be used, even unfairly, to impugn or attack your character and qualifications for a government position?

42. Do you know anyone or any organization that might take any steps, overtly or covertly, fairly or unfairly, to criticize your appointment, including any news organization? If so, please identify and explain the basis for the potential criticism.

43. Please provide any other information, including information about other members of your family, that could suggest a conflict of interest or be a possible source of embarrassment to you, your family or the President.

APPENDIX 2

EDWARD M. KENNEDY, MASSACHUSETTS, CHAIRMAN

CLAIBORNE PELL, RHODE ISLAND   NANCY LANDON KASSEBAUM, KANSAS
HOWARD M. METZENBAUM, OHIO   JAMES M. JEFFORDS, VERMONT
CHRISTOPHER J. DODD, CONNECTICUT DAN COATS, INDIANA
PAUL SIMON, ILLINOIS   JUDD GREGG, NEW HAMPSHIRE
TOM HARKIN, IOWA   STROM THURMOND, SOUTH CAROLINA
BARBARA A. MIKULSKI, MARYLAND ORRIN G. HATCH, UTAH
JEFF BINGAMAN, NEW MEXICO DAVE DURENBERGER, MINNESOTA
PAUL D. WELLSTONE, MINNESOTA
HARRIS WOFFORD, PENNSYLVANIA

NICK LITTLEFIELD, STAFF DIRECTOR AND CHIEF COUNSEL
SUSAN K. HATTAN, MINORITY STAFF DIRECTOR

United States Senate

COMMITTEE ON LABOR AND
HUMAN RESOURCES

WASHINGTON, DC 20510-6300

April 5, 1993

Department of Labor
200 Constitution Avenue, NW
F1325
Washington, D.C. 20210

Dear

Your name has been referred to the Committee on Labor and Human Resources to be Assistant Secretary of Labor.

As required by the committee's rules of procedure, the committee respectfully requests that you complete the enclosed form. Please observe that the form is in two parts:

Part I requests information relating to your employment history, education, and background. Your responses to those questions will be made public.

Part II requests financial and other background data. Your responses to Part II will not be made public unless the committee determines that it bears directly on your qualifications to be Assistant Secretary.

The committee would appreciate your completing the form and returning it to me at your convenience. Please note that page 10 requires your signature, sworn and subscribed before a notary.

Sincerely,

Nick Littlefield
Staff Director and Chief Counsel

P.S. On occasion, nominees have not responded to "Political affiliations and activities ... during the last _five_ years," on page 3 (see page 183 of this volume). Certain members of the committee will not consider nominations until the statement is completed in its entirety, including specific candidates and amounts of contributions.

Enclosure

STATEMENT FOR COMPLETION BY PRESIDENTIAL NOMINEES

PART 1: ALL THE INFORMATION IN THIS PART WILL BE MADE PUBLIC

Name: _____ _____ _____
             (LAST)   (FIRST)   (OTHER)

Position to which   Date of
nominated: _____ nomination: _____

Date of birth: _____ Place of birth: _____
      (DAY) (MONTH) (YEAR)

Marital status: Full name of spouse:

Name and ages
  of children: _____ _____ _____

               _____ _____ _____

               _____ _____ _____

Education:	Institution	Dates attended	Degrees received	Dates of degrees
	_____	_____	_____	_____
	_____	_____	_____	_____
	_____	_____	_____	_____
	_____	_____	_____	_____
	_____	_____	_____	_____

Honors and awards: List below all scholarships, fellowships, honorary
    degrees, military medals, honorary society memberships, and
    any other special recognitions for outstanding service or
    achievement.

_____

_____

_____

_____

_____

_____

Memberships: List below all memberships and offices held in professional, fraternal, business, scholarly, civic, charitable and other organizations for the last five years and any other prior memberships or offices you consider relevant.

Organization	Office held (if any)	Dates
_____	_____	_____
_____	_____	_____
_____	_____	_____
_____	_____	_____
_____	_____	_____
_____	_____	_____

Employment record: List below all positions held since college, including the title or description of job, name of employer, location of work, and dates of inclusive employment.

_____

_____

_____

_____

_____

_____

_____

_____

_____

_____

_____

Government
experience: List any advisory, consultative, honorary or other part-time
              service or positions with Federal, State, or local governments
              other than those listed above.

_____

_____

_____

_____

_____

Published
writings: List the titles, publishers and dates of books, articles, reports
              or other published materials you have written.

_____

_____

_____

_____

_____

Political
affiliations
and activities: List all memberships and offices held in or financial
              contributions and services rendered to all political parties or
              election committees during the last five years.

_____

_____

_____

_____

_____

Future
employment
relationships: 1. Indicate whether you will sever all connections with your
present employer, business firm, association or organi-
zation if you are confirmed by the Senate.

2. State whether you have any plans after completing
government service to resume employment, affiliation or
practice with your previous employer, business firm,
association or organization.

3. Has a commitment been made to you for employment
after you leave Federal service?

4. Do you intend to serve the full term for which you have
been appointed or until the next Presidential election,
whichever is applicable?

Potential
conflicts
of interest: 1. Describe any financial arrangements, deferred compensation agreements or other continuing financial, business
or professional dealings with business associates, clients
or customers who will be affected by policies which you
will influence in the position to which you have been
nominated.

_____

_____

_____

2. List any investments, obligations, liabilities, or other financial relationships which constitute potential conflicts of
interest with the position to which you have been
nominated.

_____

_____

_____

3. Describe any business relationship, dealing or financial transaction which you have had during the last five years whether for yourself, on behalf of a client, or acting as an agent, that constitutes a potential conflict of interest with the position to which you have been nominated.

_____

_____

_____

_____

_____

4. List any lobbying activity during the past 10 years in which you have engaged for the purpose of directly or indirectly influencing the passage, defeat or modification of any Federal legislation or of affecting the administration and execution of Federal law or policy.

_____

_____

_____

_____

5. Explain how you will resolve any potential conflict of interest that may be disclosed by your responses to the above items.

_____

_____

_____

_____

PART II: INFORMATION IN THIS PART WILL BE DISCLOSED WHEN THE COMMITTEE DETERMINES THAT IT BEARS DIRECTLY ON YOUR QUALIFICATIONS TO HOLD THE POSITION TO WHICH YOU HAVE BEEN NOMINATED

FINANCIAL STATEMENT

NET WORTH

Provide a complete, current financial net worth statement which itemizes in detail all assets (including bank accounts, real estate, securities, trusts, investments, and other financial holdings) all liabilities (including debts, mortgages, loans, and other financial obligations) of yourself, your spouse, and other immediate family members of your household.

ASSETS			LIABILITIES		
Cash on hand and in banks			Notes payable to banks—secured		
U.S. Government securities—add			Notes payable to banks—unsecured		
schedule—			Notes payable to relatives		
Listed securities—add schedule			Notes payable to others		
Unlisted securities—add schedule			Accounts and bills due		
Accounts and notes receivable:			Unpaid income tax		
Due from relatives and friends			Other unpaid tax and interest		
Due from others			Real estate mortgages payable—add		
Doubtful			schedule		
Real estate owned—add schedule			Chattel mortgages and other liens		
Real estate mortgages receivable			payable		
Autos and other personal property			Other debts—itemize:		
Cash value—life insurance					
Other assets—itemize:					
			Total liabilities		
			Net worth		
			Total liabilities		
Total assets			and net worth		

CONTINGENT LIABILITIES			GENERAL INFORMATION		
As endorser, comaker or guarantor			Are any assets pledged?		
On leases or contracts			(Add schedule.)		
Legal Claims			Are you defendant in any suits or		
Provision for Federal Income Tax			legal actions?		
Other special debt			Have you ever taken bankruptcy?		

SOURCES OF INCOME LAST 3 YEARS

1. List sources and amounts of all income received during the last 3 years, including all salaries, fees, dividends, interest, gifts, rents, royalties, patents, honoraria, and other items exceeding $500 or more. (If you prefer to do so, copies of U.S. income tax returns for these years may be substituted here, but their submission is not required.)

	19...	19...	19...
Salary			
Fees, royalties			
Dividends			
Interest			
Gifts			
Rents			
Other—exceeding $500			
Total			

2. List sources, amounts and dates of all anticipated receipts from deferred income arrangements, stock options, uncompleted contracts and other future benefits which you expect to derive from previous business relationships, professional services and firm memberships or from former employers, clients, and customers.

Affiliations:

> List the names of all corporations, companies, firms, or other business enterprises, partnerships, nonprofit organizations, and educational or other institutions:
>
> > —with which you are now connected as an employee, officer, owner, director, trustee, partner, advisor, attorney, or consultant. Any listed relationship or affiliation that you wish to continue during the term of your appointment should be noted with an asterisk.
> >
> > —in which you have any financial interest through the ownership of stocks, stock options, bonds, partnership interests, or other securities, which you wish to retain during your period of government service should be noted with an asterisk.

Personal Data: 1. Have your tax returns been the subject of any audit or investigation or inquiry at any time by Federal, State or local authorities, which resulted in a tax lien or other collection procedure?

_____

_____

_____

2. Have you ever been convicted for violation of any Federal, State, county or municipal law, regulation or ordinance? If so, please give full details (do not include traffic violations for which a fine of $100 or less was imposed).

_____

_____

3. Are you currently under Federal, State, or local investigation of you for a possible violation of a criminal statute? If so, please provide full details.

_____

_____

4. Have you ever been disciplined or cited for a breach of ethics or unprofessional conduct by, or are you currently the subject of a formal complaint procedure in any court, administrative agency, professional association, disciplinary committee, or other professional group? If so, please give full details.

_____

_____

5. Have you ever been involved in civil litigation, or administrative, regulatory or legislative investigation of any kind, either as plaintiff, defendant, respondent, witness or party in interest, which may have a material effect on the position for which you are being considered?

_____

_____

_____

AFFIDAVIT:

)ss

, being duly sworn, hereby states that
he/she has read and signed the foregoing Financial Statement and that
the information provided therein is, to the best of his/her knowledge and
belief, current, accurate, and complete.

_____

Subscribe and sworn before me this   day of   , 19

_____

Notary Public

APPENDIX 3

TAX CHECK WAIVER

I am signing this waiver to permit the Internal Revenue Service to release information about me which would otherwise be confidential. This information will be used in connection with my appointment or employment by the United States Government. This waiver is made pursuant to 26 U.S.C. 6103(c).

I request that the Internal Revenue Service send the information to: President Clinton and the Office of Counsel to the President, acting on behalf of the President.

The information I wish released is:

1.   Have I failed to file any Federal income tax return which was required to be filed for any of the last three years?

If this waiver is received by the Internal Revenue Service before July 1, the "last three years" shall mean the latest three years for which information is available, since the return for the immediate last year may not have been processed.

2.   Were any of these returns filed more than 45 days after the due date for filing (determined with regard to any extension of time for filing)?

3.   Have I failed to pay any tax, penalty or interest during the last three years within 45 days of the date on which the Internal Revenue Service gave notice of the amount due and demanded payment?

4.   Has any penalty for negligence under Section 6655(a) of the Internal Revenue Code been assessed against me this year or during the last three years?

5.   Am I or have I ever been under investigation by the Internal Revenue Service for possible criminal offenses, and what were the results of such investigation(s)?

6.   Has any civil penalty for fraud been assessed against me?

If the information which is to be released includes a "YES" answer to any of the above six questions, I authorize the Internal Revenue Service to release any information relative to that question.

To help the Internal Revenue Service find my tax records, I am voluntarily giving the following information:

MY NAME _____   MY SS#: _____

IF MARRIED AND FILED A JOINT RETURN:

    HUSBAND/WIFE NAME: _____

    HUSBAND/WIFE SS#: _____

    CURRENT ADDRESS _____

NAMES AND ADDRESSES SHOWN ON RETURNS (IF DIFFERENT FROM ABOVE)

YEAR   NAME   ADDRESS

_____

_____

_____

_____

DATE: _____

        (WAIVER INVALID UNLESS RECEIVED BY
        INTERNAL REVENUE SERVICE WITHIN 60
        DAYS OF THIS DATE)

            _____

        (SIGNATURE OF TAXPAYER AUTHORIZING
        THE DISCLOSURE OF RETURN INFORMATION)

Appendix 4

THE WHITE HOUSE
WASHINGTON

MEMORANDUM FOR PROSPECTIVE APPOINTEES

FROM: OFFICE OF COUNSEL TO THE PRESIDENT

SUBJECT: Ethics Standards and Financial Report Requirements

President Clinton is committed to providing the citizens of the United States with an Administration whose officials hold themselves to the highest standards of integrity. To that end, it is important for you to be aware of the legal requirements and restrictions that apply to you in connection with your prospective employment in the Executive Office of the President.

FINANCIAL DISCLOSURE REQUIREMENTS

In addition to the forms required to initiate your security clearance, which you should already have received, two additional reports are required to facilitate your compliance with conflict-of-interest requirements.

    1.   You are required by the Ethics in Government Act of 1978 to file a financial disclosure report (SF-278) which is subject to public disclosure. This package contains two copies of the form and a sheet of helpful hints on completing the required new entrant filing.

    2.   You are required to submit a response to the Personal Data Statement Questionnaire (PDS). Your response can be on plain paper, but please sign and date it.

The PDS should be completed and returned to Clifford J. Mauton (Room 136, OEOB, 456-6229) within 1 day.

A draft of your Public Financial Disclosure Form should be completed and returned to Mr. Mauton within 4 days.

HOW TO FILL OUT
THE EXECUTIVE BRANCH PERSONNEL
PUBLIC FINANCIAL DISCLOSURE REPORT (SP 278)

Supplemental Instructions for Nominees/Appointees

The SF 278 financial disclosure report must be reviewed and certified by your agency and by the independent Office of Government Ethics (OGE) (prior to its submission to the Senate, if Senate confirmed).

Incomplete or incorrectly filled out forms cannot be certified. You should, therefore, complete the form carefully in accordance with the printed instructions. The additional instructions below are intended to help you avoid the most common problems.

If you have any questions about filling out this form, please contact Kathleen Whalen, Assistant Counsel to the President, at (202) 456-7900.

GENERAL INSTRUCTIONS

Please type or print your responses. Complete all sections in Schedules A, C, and D. You should check the "NONE" box if you have nothing to report. You should indicate "Nominee — not applicable" in Parts I and II of Schedule B, which is for incumbent and termination filers only.

(NOTE: if you are already a Government employee subject to SF 278 reporting requirements, and you are filling out the nominee form between January 1 and May 15, you may use the same form for the incumbent report due May 15 for the prior calendar year. If you do so, you should also complete Schedule B, and check both the "Incumbent" and "Nominee" boxes on the cover page.)

Please do not leave any section blank. If you do not check the "NONE" box (or write "Nominee — not applicable" on Schedule B), someone will have to contact you for clarification, which will slow up the nomination process.

Be sure to provide required information for your spouse and dependent children.

If you need additional space, you may photocopy any schedule.

SPECIFIC INSTRUCTIONS

1. Cover Page

You must sign and date page 1. (An attorney, accountant or other person may not sign for you.) Please provide a current telephone number where you can be contacted for additional or clarifying information.

2. Schedule A — Assets and Income

a. Reporting Period

The reporting period for Schedule A is the preceding calendar year and the present year up to the closing date. (Choose a closing date which is within the 30-day period prior to the date you sign and file the form).

b. Assets and Income Sources

Report all assets that are owned by you, your spouse or dependent children for investment or income-producing purposes which had a fair market value as of the closing date of more than $1,000. ALSO report all sources of earned, investment and non-investment income that yielded more than $200 in income during the reporting period.

The reporting threshold for your spouse's earned income is $1,000. The name and address of your spouse's employer and the type of work performed should be identified. You need not report the exact amount of a spouse's salary.

Some examples of reportable items:

—stocks
—bonds
—real property
—gold
—art bought for investment purposes
—debts owed to you, except by relatives
—annuities
—futures contracts
—mutual funds
—assets in your IRA
—commercial animals
—crops
—a vested beneficial interest in a trust
—fees
—salaries

—commissions
—honoraria
—partnership income

Interest-bearing checking and savings accounts and other bank deposits or certificates of deposit must be reported if the interest exceeds $200 in the reporting period OR if the total in any one institution is over $5,000.

C. What to show on the form

(1) Give a description of the asset or source of income and check the type of income and the category of amount of income. For financial institutions, real property and partnerships, include an address. Where a partnership is reported, you should indicate if you are a limited or general partner, and identify the nature of the business.

2) DO NOT USE ABBREVIATIONS. Mutual funds, company names and names of stocks should be spelled out completely.

(3) Rental property — Gross rental income (before any deductions for depreciation/maintenance) should be reported. Mortgages over $10,000 on rental property must be reported on Schedule C. If the mortgage is below the reporting limit or if there is no mortgage, please so indicate.

(4) Mutual Funds — the name of the investment firm as well as the specific fund must be reported (e.g., Merrill Lynch Basic Value Fund). If a fund is devoted to particular economic or geographic sector, the sector should be indicated.

(5) IRAs — If an IRA contains other than cash, the assets must be identified. Although interest/dividend income is reinvested rather than distributed to you, it must nonetheless be reported as income to you.

(6) Keoghs - In most cases, you will need to list and value separately each of the assets held in the plan. You will also need to indicate whether you determine the investments in the Keogh or whether the plan is independently managed. If it is independently managed, indicate if you can, the entity that manages the plan. If a plan is both independently managed and widely diversified (such that not more than 5 percent of its holdings are issued by any one non-U.S.-government issuer and not more than 20 percent of its holdings are in any one economic or geographic sector), then you will not be required to list the sub-assets of the plan but should instead state that the plan is independently managed and widely diversified.

(7) Accounts with Stockbrokers — Each individual security in the account must be reported separately.

(8) <u>Private investment pools</u> — Each portfolio holding should be specifically identified and valued.

(9) <u>Trusts</u> — The individual holdings and income of any trust in which there is a vested beneficial income or remainder interest must be reported, unless the trust is an excepted trust or specifically approved by the Office of Government Ethics as a qualified trust.

(10) <u>Assets that Have Been Sold</u> — You are reporting the value or the asset at the close of the reporting period. If you no longer hold the asset, but you did receive more than $200 in income from the asset during the reporting period, check the "none (or less than $1,001)" box in block B and indicate that the item was sold. Also complete block C (see (12) below).

(11) <u>"Other" Income</u> — If you are reporting income that is <u>not</u> from dividends, rent, interest, capital gains, or an excepted or qualified trust, indicate the type of income in the "Other" column, and give the <u>exact</u> amount of income in the column labeled "Actual Amount Only if 'Other' Specified" (e.g., Partnership income - $9,382).

(12) <u>More Than One Type of Income</u> — Some items may generate more than one type of income (e.g., rent and capital gain income for a rental property sold during the reporting period). Check two (or more) boxes for the category of income and the total of the category of amount.

(13) <u>Employee benefit plans</u> — Each plan must be specifically identified. For each plan, indicate if it is independently managed or self-directed. If it is independently managed, include if you can the name of the managing institution.

3.   <u>Schedule B - Transactions and Gifts, Reimbursements and Travel Expenses</u>

If you are <u>not</u> currently in a government position in which you are required to file an SP 278, you should indicate "Nominee — not applicable" at the top of Schedule B and skip to the instructions for Schedule C, on the next page.

If you currently are in a government position in which you are required to file an SP 278 and you wish to use this report as a combined annual and nominee report, you must complete Schedule B.

a. Part I — <u>Transactions</u>

Describe any purchase, sale or exchange by you, your spouse or dependent children of any investment or income-producing asset during the reporting period if the value of the transaction exceeded $1,000. If an exchange was made, indicate which assets were involved.

If an asset was sold and there was no reportable (i.e., over $200) capital gain or other income to include on Schedule A, you should indicate "no reportable income" after the entry on this schedule. Also indicate whether it was a total or partial sale.

In addition, you should explain why any assets reported in your last report are not reported this year, to make it clear that you did not simply forget them. It is sufficient to say: "ABC and XYZ stock are not reportable because income and value are below reporting limits."

    b. Part II — Gifts, Reimbursements and Travel Expenses

In the description of the gift/reimbursement: identify the source (if a company or organization is involved, describe the nature of its business); indicate the purpose of any travel; provide the title or subject of any speech; describe the donor's relationship to you and whether the donor has any connection with a foreign government or your agency; describe the occasion or purpose for which any gift was given.

4.   Schedule C — Liabilities and Agreements and Arrangements

    a. Part I — Liabilities

You must include the name and address of the creditor, the type of liability, the date, term and interest rate, and the highest value of the liability during the reporting period. When reporting a mortgage (for rental or business property; not for personal residences that are not rented out), you should indicate for which property listed on Schedule A the mortgage is held.

    b. Part II — Agreements or Arrangements

(1) Describe all agreements or arrangements (not just those entered into during the reporting period) concerning future employment, leaves of absence, severance payments, continuing payments from a former employer, or continuing participation in employee pension, welfare or benefit plans (except those with the United States Government).

(2) Note that any such payments must also be reported on Schedule A.

(3) Specifically identify any present positions which will be terminated upon entry into government service.

(5)   Schedule D — Positions Held Outside U.S. Government and Compensation in Excess of $5,000 Paid by One Source

The reporting for Schedule D is the preceding <u>two</u> calendar years and the current year up to the closing date.

a. Part I — Positions Held Outside U.S. Government

Report and describe positions held by you in any for-profit or non-profit organization at any time during the reporting period. Be sure to include any partnership position you may hold. Include <u>both</u> paid and unpaid positions and indicate whether each one is paid or unpaid. If you received more than $200 in compensation, you must report this income on Schedule A.

Positions with a religious, social, fraternal or political entity and positions of a solely honorary nature do not have to be reported.

b. Part II —Compensation in Excess of $5,000 Paid by One Source

Report the source of income and nature of services performed where you received more than $5000 in compensation. U.S. Government income need not be reported. You must include in this part a listing of clients of a firm if the firm received more than $5,000 in compensation for services you provided.

Appendix 5

THE WHITE HOUSE
WASHINGTON

MEMORANDUM FOR PROSPECTIVE APPOINTEES

FROM: OFFICE OF COUNSEL TO THE PRESIDENT

This memorandum confirms in writing your express consent for the Federal Bureau of Investigation to investigate your background or conduct appropriate file reviews in connection with the consideration of your application for employment.

The FBI investigation will include the collection and use of relevant information concerning your personal history, and it is necessary that you authorize the disclosure of such information to the FBI. Information may be disseminated outside the FBI when necessary to fulfill obligations imposed by law.

By volunteering information concerning activities protected by the First Amendment, it will be assumed that you are expressly authorizing the maintenance of this information in the records of any Federal agency.

If you consent to such inquiries, please sign your name below and return this original memorandum of consent to this office.

Name (please print or type) _____

Signature _____ Date _____

APPENDIX 6

THE WHITE HOUSE
WASHINGTON

ACKNOWLEDGEMENT AND CONSENT
REGARDING INTENT TO NOMINATE OR APPOINT

The undersigned acknowledges and agrees to the following:

1. The undersigned (the "Prospective Nominee"), by his or her signature below, acknowledges and consents to consideration by the President of the United States for appointment or nomination to a position within the Executive Branch.

2. The Prospective Nominee agrees that, following completion of a preliminary investigation into the Prospective Nominee's background using procedures established by the office of Counsel to the President, the Prospective Nominee may be identified publicly as a person the President intends to nominate for appointment to a position in the Executive Branch, and consents to such identification.

3. The Prospective Nominee further agrees that, notwithstanding such identification: (i) the Prospective Nominee will not, at such time, have actually been nominated by the President; (ii) an investigation into the personal and financial background of the Nominee will continue, including but not limited to completion of an investigation by the FBI and the Senate if the Prospective Nominee is subject to Senate confirmation; (iii) the Prospective Nominee will have no vested interest of any kind in the position for which he or she is considered; (iv) consideration of the Prospective Nominee may be withdrawn at any time by the President; and (v) upon completion of all investigation into the Prospective Nominee's background, the Prospective Nominee may be asked, as part of his or her confirmation or appointment, to divest certain assets, to resign certain positions, and/or to agree to recuse himself or herself from involvement in matters which may arise in the conduct of Prospective Nominee's official duties.

The Prospective Nominee, by his or her signature below, agrees to the above and foregoing.

DATED THIS_____ DAY OF_____, 1996.

_____
(signature of Prospective Nominee)

_____
(social security number)

201

APPENDIX 7

Instructions for Completing SF 278

I. Introduction

Reporting Periods

Incumbents: Complete Schedules A, B, C, and Part I of D. The reporting period is the preceding calendar year, except Part II of Schedule C and Part I of Schedule D where you must also include any positions held and agreements or arrangements made from the beginning of the filing year until the date you file. Schedule B need not include transactions made, or gifts or reimbursements received, during a period when the filer was not a Federal employee.

Termination Filers: Complete Schedules A, B, C, and Part I of D. The reporting period begins at the end of the period covered by your previous filing and ends at the date of termination of Government employment in the position.

Nominees, New Entrants, and Candidates for President and Vice President: Complete Schedules A, C, and D (candidates do not file Part II of Schedule D), as follows:

Schedule A — The reporting period for income (BLOCK C) is the preceding calendar year up to the date of filing. Value assets in BLOCK B as of any date you choose that is less than 31 days before the date of filing.

Schedule C, Part I (Liabilities) — The reporting period is the preceding calendar year and the current calendar year up to any date you choose that is less than 31 days before the date of filing.
Schedule C, Part II (Agreements or Arrangements)—Show any agreements or arrangements as of the date of filing.

Schedule D — The reporting period is the preceding two calendar years and the current calendar year up to the date of filing.

Scope of Disclosure

The extent of the reporting requirement is noted in each schedule. In addition to your individual financial information, you are required to report information concerning your spouse and dependent children in several schedules of the form. However, no report is required with respect to your spouse if he or she is living separate and apart from you with the intention of terminating the marriage or providing for permanent separation. In addition, no report is required with respect to any income or obligations of an individual arising from the dissolution of marriage or permanent separation from a spouse. There are other exceptions to the reporting of assets and income, transactions, and liabilities of a spouse or dependent child which are discussed in the instructions applicable to those subjects.

A basic premise of the statutory financial disclosure requirements is that those having responsibility for review of reports filed pursuant to the Act or permitted public access to reports must be given sufficient information by reporting individuals concerning the nature of their outside interests and activities so that an informed judgment can be made with respect to compliance with applicable conflict of interest laws and standards of conduct regulations. Therefore, it is important that you carefully complete the attached form. This report is a safeguard for you as well as the Government, in that it provides a mechanism for determining actual or potential conflicts between your public responsibilities and your private interests and activities and allows you and your agency to fashion appropriate protections against such conflicts when they first appear.

A Presidential nominee to a position requiring the advice and consent of the Senate shall file with the Senate committee considering the nomination an amendment to the initial report, which shall update all items of earned income and honoraria through the period ending no earlier than 5 days before the scheduled date of the Senate committee hearing on the nomination. This update shall be provided in the manner requested by the Senate committee considering the nomination. Copies shall be provided to OGE and your agency ethics official.

Definition of Terms

- **Category of Amount**

Reportable financial interests are disclosed either by actual amount or by category of amount, depending on the interest, as specified by the form. You may, but you are not required to, indicate an actual amount where the form provides for a category of amount or value.

- **Dependent Child**

The term "dependent child" means your son, daughter, stepson, or stepdaughter if such a person is either: (1) unmarried, under age 21, and living in your household, or (2) a "dependent" of yours within the meaning of section 152 of the Internal Revenue Code of 1986.

- **Excepted Investment Fund**

An excepted investment fund is a mutual fund, common trust fund of a bank, pension or deferred compensation plan, or any other investment fund, which is widely held; publicly traded (or available) or widely-diversified; and under circumstances where you neither exercise control over nor have the ability to exercise control over the financial interest held by the fund. A fund is widely diversified when it holds no more than 5% of the value of its portfolio in the securities of any one issuer (other than the U.S. Government) and no more than 20% in any particular economic or geographic sector.

- **Gifts**

See instructions for Schedule B, Part II.B.

- **Honoraria**

The term "honoraria" means payments of money or anything of value to you or your spouse for an appearance, speech, or article, excluding necessary travel expenses. See 5 CFR Part 2636.

- **Personal Savings Account**

The term "personal savings account" includes a certificate of deposit, a money market account, or any other form of deposit in a bank, savings and loan association, credit union, or similar financial institution.

- **Relative**

The term "relative" means an individual who is your father, mother, son, daughter, brother, sister, uncle, aunt, great uncle, great aunt, first cousin, nephew, niece, husband, wife, grandfather, grandmother, grandson, granddaughter, father-in-law, mother-in-law, son-in-law, daughter-in-law, brother-in-law, sister-in-law, stepfather, stepmother, stepson, stepdaughter, stepbrother, stepsister, half brother, half sister, your spouse's grandfather or grandmother, or your fiance or fiancee.

- **Trusts ("Qualified" and "Excepted")**

See instructions for Schedule A, Part II.B., and 5 CFR Part 2634, Subpart D.

- **Value**

You may use any one of the methods described below, in determining fair market value:

Option 1 — any good faith estimate of the value of the property if the exact value is unknown or not easily obtainable;

Option 2 — value based upon a recent appraisal of the property interest;

Option 3 — the purchase price of your property interest, or estimated retail price of a gift;

Option 4 — the assessed value of the property for tax purposes, adjusted to reflect current market value if the tax assessment is computed at less than 100% value;

Option 5 — the year-end book value of non-publicly traded stock, or the year-end exchange value of corporate stocks, or the face value of corporate bonds or comparable securities;

Option 6 — the net worth of your interest (as in a business partnership or other jointly held business interest);

Option 7 — the equity value of your interest (as in a solely owned business or commercial enterprise); or

Option 8 — exact value (e.g., personal savings accounts) or any other recognized indication of value (such as last sale on a stock exchange).

II. Who Must File

a. Candidates for nomination or election to the office of President or Vice President.

b. Presidential nominees to positions requiring the advice and consent of the Senate, other than those nominated for judicial office or as a Foreign Service Officer or for appointment to a rank in the uniformed services at a pay grade of 0–6, or below.

c. The following newly elected or appointed officials:

- The President;

- The Vice President;

- Officers and employees (including special Government employees, as defined in 18 U.S.C. § 202) whose positions are classified above GS–15 of the General Schedule or the rate of basic pay for which is fixed, other than under the General Schedule, at a rate equal to or greater than 120% of the minimum rate of basic pay for GS–15 of the General Schedule.

- Members of the uniformed services in pay grade 0–7 or above;

• Officers or employees in any other positions determined by the Director of the Office of Government Ethics to be of equal classification to above GS–15;

• Administrative law judges;

• Employees in the excepted service in positions which are of a confidential or policy-making character, unless by regulation their positions have been excluded by the Director of the Office of Government Ethics.

• The Postmaster General, the Deputy Postmaster General, each Governor of the Board of Governors of the U.S. Postal Service and officers or employees of the U.S. Postal Service or Postal Rate Commission in positions for which the rate of basic pay is equal to or greater than 120% of the minimum rate of basic pay for GS–15 of the General Schedule.

• The Director of the Office of Government Ethics and each designated agency ethics official; and

• Civilian employees in the Executive Office of the President (other than special Government employees) who hold commissions of appointment from the President.

d. Incumbent officials holding positions referred to in section II.c. of these instructions if they have served 61 days or more in the position during the preceding calendar year.

e. Officials who have terminated employment after having served 61 days or more in a calendar year in a position referred to in section II.c. and have not accepted another such position within 30 days thereafter.

III. When to File

a. Within 30 days after becoming a candidate for nomination or election to the office of President or Vice President, or by May 15 of that calendar year, whichever is later, but at least 30 days before the election, and on or before May 15 of each succeeding year an individual continues to be a candidate.

b. At any time after the President or President-elect has publicly announced an intention to nominate an individual referred to in section II.b. of these instructions, but no later than 5 days after the President transmits the nomination to the Senate.

c. Within 30 days after assuming a position described in section II.c. unless such an individual has left another such position within 30 days prior to assuming the new position, or has already filed a report with respect to nomination for the new position (section II.b.) or as a candidate for the position (section II.a.).

d. No later than May 15th annually, in the case of those in a position described in section II.d.

e. In the event an individual terminates employment in the position and does not accept another position described in section II.c. within 30 days, the report must be filed no later than the 30th day after termination.

IV. Where to File

a. Candidates for President and Vice President, with the Federal Election Commission.

b. The President and Vice President, with the Office of Government Ethics.

c. Members of a uniformed service, with the Service Secretary concerned.

d. All others, with the designated agency ethics official, or that official's delegate, at the agency in which the individual serves, will serve or has served.

e. In the case of individuals nominated by or to be nominated by the President to positions requiring confirmation of the Senate, see 5 CFR Part 2634 for expedited procedures and filing location.

V. General Instructions

a. This form consists of the front page and four Schedules. You must complete each Part of all Schedules as required. If you have no information to report in any Part of a Schedule, you should indicate "None." If you are not required to complete Schedule B or Part II of Schedule D, you should leave it blank. Schedule A combines a report of income items with the disclosure of certain property interests. Schedule B deals with transactions in real property or certain other assets, as well as gifts and reimbursements. Schedules C and D relate to liabilities and employment relationships. After completing the first page and each Part of the Schedules (including extra sheets of any Schedule where continuation pages are required for any Part), consecutively number all pages.

b. The information to be disclosed is only that which the Ethics in Government Act of 1978, as amended, and 5 CFR Part 2634 specifically require. You may, however, include any additional information, beyond those requirements, that you wish to disclose for purposes of clarification. Disclosure of information does not authorize any holdings, income, honoraria, liabilities, transactions, gifts, reimbursements, affiliations or positions otherwise prohibited by law, Executive order, rule or regulation.

c. Combine on one form the information applicable to yourself, your spouse and dependent children; or if more convenient, use separate schedules to report the required information applicable to family members. You may, if you desire, distinguish any entry for a family member by preceding the entry with an (S) if it is for a spouse or a (DC) if it pertains to a dependent child. Joint assets may be indicated by a (J). See 5 CFR Part 2634, Subpart C, for exclusions in the case of separation or divorce.

d. Definitions of the various terms used in these instructions and detailed information as to what is required to be disclosed are contained in 5 CFR Part 2634.

e. In the case of references to entities which are operating trades or businesses which do not have listed securities, you must provide sufficient information about these private entities to give the reviewers of your disclosure report an adequate basis for the conflicts analysis required by the Act. Thus, you must disclose the location and primary trade or business of private entities, as well as attributed interests and activities not solely incidental to such a primary trade or business. For instance, if your family swimming pool services corporation incurs a liability to purchase an apartment house for investment in addition to its pool services business, you will have to report the apartment house investment as part of the nature of the business of the family corporation.

f. In the case of references to entities which are investment funds such as mutual or pension funds (whether public or private), you must disclose the portfolio holdings and all other items such as transactions and liabilities to the extent otherwise required for reportable interests, unless the entity is an "excepted investment fund." See Definition of Terms above.

g. If you need assistance in completing this form, contact the designated agency ethics official of the agency in which you serve, will serve, or have served.

Schedule A

I. General Instructions

Two of the general disclosure requirements of the Act concern certain interests in property (generally referred to here as assets) and items of income. Schedule A is designed to enable you to meet both of these reporting requirements. Generally a description of your, your spouse's, and your dependent child's assets and sources of income is required to be listed in BLOCK A of the Schedule. Reading from left to right across the page from each description of the asset or income source, you will be able to report in BLOCK B the value of each asset, and in BLOCK C the type and amount of income generated by that asset or received from the non-asset source.

On Schedule A are four examples which are representative of the reporting scheme of this Schedule. The first example represents the proper method of reporting stock of Central Airlines Company held at the end of the reporting period which then had a value of $75,000. The individual had also received dividends of $1,500, reported in BLOCK C. If the Central Airlines stock had been sold, there would be a check in the "None (or less than $ 1,001)" column in BLOCK B if the individual no longer owned any of the stock at the end of the reporting period, and there would be an entry for capital gains as well as dividends in BLOCK C if they were realized during the period. The second example represents the proper method of reporting the source of $130,000 of earned income from private law practice, as well as $18,500 the reporting individual maintained in the capital account in the law firm at the end of the reporting period.

The third example represents acceptable reporting of an investment fund which is widely held, widely diversified (or publicly traded) and independently managed. Because it meets these requirements, no individual assets of the fund need to be reported, and the type of income does not need to be broken into dividends, interest, or capital gains as long as the column for "excepted investment fund" is marked. The fourth example reports a mutual fund held in an IRA from which the filer has accrued dividends of $10,000.

Normally you will have to list an item only once in BLOCK A with all other value and income information associated with that item shown on the same line to the right. However, when you have a number of different kinds of financial arrangements and income involving one entity, a full disclosure of all the required information for that entity may require more than one line. You may always use more than one line for clarification if you choose.

II. Property Interests and Assets

(BLOCKS A and B)

A. Items to Report

Report the identity and category of valuation of any interest in property (real or personal) held by **you, your spouse or dependent child** in a trade or business, or for investment or the production of income which has a fair market value which **exceeds $1,000** as of the close of the reporting period. These interests include, but are not limited to, stocks, bonds, pension interests and annuities, futures contracts, mutual funds, IRA assets, tax shelters, beneficial interests in trusts, personal savings or other bank accounts, real estate, commercial crops, livestock, accounts or other funds receivable, and collectible items held for resale or investment. **Exceptions:** Exclude your personal residence (unless rented out) and any personal liability owed to you, your spouse or dependent child by a spouse or dependent child, or by a parent, brother, sister or child of you, your spouse, or dependent child. Exclude any retirement benefits (including the Thrift Savings Plan) from Federal Government employment and any social security benefits. Exclude also any deposits aggregating $5,000 or less in personal savings accounts in a single financial institution.

With respect to assets of a spouse or a dependent child, do not report items:

(1) which represent your spouse's or dependent child's sole financial interest or responsibility and of which you have no knowledge;

(2) which are not in any way, past or present, derived from your income, assets, or activities; and

(3) from which you neither derive, nor expect to derive, any financial or economic benefit.

Note: It is very difficult for most individuals to meet all three parts of this test especially (3). For instance, if you file a joint tax return with your spouse, you derive a financial or economic benefit from the items involved and you are charged with knowledge of those items. A trust for the education of your minor child would also convey a financial benefit to you. Therefore, those asset and income items do not fit the test.

A personal residence held for investment or production of income, such as a summer home rented during parts of the year, must be reported.

Intermittent sales from personal property such as collections of antiques or art holdings demonstrate that the items are held for investment or the production of income and should therefore be reported.

B. What to Show on the Form

Enter the identity of the asset in BLOCK A and then show the value in BLOCK B. **Only the category of value, rather than the actual value of the property interest or asset,** must be shown. You need not disclose which valuation methods you used.

For assets such as stocks, bonds, and securities, report any holdings directly held or attributable to **you, your spouse or dependent child** from one source totaling more than $1,000 in value. **Identify the holding and show the category of value.** If you hold different types of securities of the same corporation (e.g., bonds and stocks of "X" Corporation), these holdings should be considered as being from the same source for purposes of determining whether the aggregate value of the interest is below or above the $1,000 threshold value. Report personal savings accounts only if they aggregate more than $5,000 in a single financial institution.

If you have an interest in an investment fund or pool which is an "excepted investment fund" (see Definition of Terms above), you need only identify the interest by giving the complete name of the fund, rather than identifying the underlying assets as well.

To report interests of you, your spouse, or dependent child in a business, a partnership, or joint venture, or the ownership of property held for investment or the production of income, identify the character of the ownership interest, and the nature and location of the business or interest, unless it is a publicly traded security. For example, the entry for a holding of farm land might show, under BLOCK A... "sole ownership of 100 acres of unimproved dairy farmland on Rural Route #1 at Pine Bluff, Madison County, Wisconsin."

You must disclose the primary trade or business of non-public entities, as well as interests and activities not solely incidental to such a trade or business. For example, if your family is involved in a private real estate investment business but as a side interest buys stock through the business in a bank, you must disclose that in addition to real estate (by type and general location), the family business holds an interest in a bank.

For an IRA (Individual Retirement Account), indicate the value of each underlying asset, as well as the income derived therefrom (even though deferred for Federal tax purposes) in accordance with section IV below, to enable the reviewer to evaluate compliance with applicable laws and regulations. If the IRA were invested solely in a mutual fund such as "Templeton World Fund, Inc." and the investment properly disclosed in Schedule A, that would be sufficient identification of the asset, since for most reporting individuals that fund would be an "excepted investment fund." If, however, the IRA had an individual or privately managed portfolio, detailed disclosure of the portfolio would be required on Schedule A in the same amount of detail as if each investment were directly held.

With respect to trusts in which a vested beneficial interest in principal or income is held, report trust interests and trust assets which had a value in excess of $1,000. See 5 CFR Part 2634 for more information about vested interests.

You need not report the identity of assets of a trust of which you, your spouse or dependent children are the beneficiaries if the interest is:

1. a "qualified blind trust" or "qualified diversified trust," which has been certified by the Office of Government Ethics, in accordance with 5 CFR Part 2634, Subpart D, or

2. an "excepted trust," that is, one which:

    A. was not created by you or your spouse or dependent children, and

    B. has holdings or sources of income of which you, your spouse and dependent children have no knowledge.

In the case of these special types of trusts, you should show in BLOCK A the identity of the trust, including the date of creation, and in BLOCK C, the classification of the trust as a "qualified trust" or an "excepted trust." (The category of amount of the trust income, if it exceeded $200, must also be reported in BLOCK C, in accordance with section IV below.)

Note: You are not permitted by the statute to "create" an excepted trust by instructing a trustee not to divulge information or otherwise avoiding previous sources of knowledge upon entering Government service.

Do not report a trust of which your spouse or dependent child is a beneficiary that meets the three part test set forth in the second paragraph under II.A. A trust that does not fit that exception may still be an excepted trust under this section; in such case, it must be reported, but the assets need not be identified.

Except for the special trusts or funds referred to above, you must identify each individual investment held by a trust or fund, which had a value in excess of $1,000. For example, in BLOCK A an entry such as "trust held by First National Bank (Boston, MA) consisting of ITT stock, U.S. Treasury certificates, and Dallas Municipal Bonds" might be made. In BLOCK B the applicable value of each trust asset would be entered. (As described under IV.B.6. Trust Income, below, the income from each asset would be entered in BLOCK C as well as income from assets of the trust sold during the reporting period.)

III. Earned and Other Non-Investment Income

(BLOCKS A and C)

A. Items to Report

For yourself, report the identity of the source in BLOCK A and the type and **actual** amount in BLOCK C of non-investment income **exceeding $200** from any one source. Such income includes fees, salaries, commissions, compensation for personal services, retirement benefits, and honoraria. Report these items on the same line as related interests in property, if any.

For your spouse, report the source, but not the amount, of non-investment income exceeding $1,000 and the source, amount and date of honoraria exceeding $200 from any one source. **No report of the earned or other non-investment income of your dependent children is required.**

Exclude for yourself and spouse income from employment by the United States Government and from any retirement system of the United States (including the Thrift Savings Plan) or from social security.

B. What to Show on the Form

1. HONORARIA — For **you or your spouse,** show honoraria aggregating more than $200 from any one source. Report the **identity of the source** in BLOCK A, and the **date** of the services performed and **actual amount** in BLOCK C. List each honorarium separately. For example, if, prior to your Government service, you received $1,500 for a speech before the Chicago Civic Club on March 19, 1991 of which $200 was actually spent for round-trip travel, and $200 went to the agent who made the speaking arrangement, on your new entrant report you would enter in BLOCK A... "Chicago Civic Club, 18 Lakeshore Dr., Chicago, IL"; in BLOCK C under OTHER (specify type)... "Honorarium"; under ACTU-AL AMOUNT... "$1,100," and under DATE... "3/19/91." Honoraria received and donated to charity must be reported, but a notation explaining that fact may be included in reporting such items. The source, date and amount of payments made or to be made directly to a charitable organization in lieu of honoraria must also be disclosed. In addition, for certain payments in lieu of honoraria you must complete a confidential report for your agency, disclosing the source, the names of charitable organization recipients, the amount, and the dates of payments, if made on or after January 1, 1991. See 5 CFR Part 2636.

2. EARNED AND OTHER NON-INVESTMENT INCOME — Include all income, exclusive of honoraria, from non-investment sources including fees, commissions, salaries, and income from personal services or retirement. Report the **identity of the source and give the actual amount of such income** exceeding $200 from any one source. For example, if you earned $450 teaching at a law school, enter in BLOCK A... "John Jones Law School, Rockville, MD"; in BLOCK C under OTHER... "Salary"; and under ACTUAL AMOUNT... "$450." If you earned $75 for teaching in one law school and $250 from teaching at another school, report only the $250 amount. Report employee benefits and severance payments which meet the reporting requirements separately from salary.

If **your spouse** has earned income in excess of $1,000 (other than honoraria) from any one source, **identify the source but show nothing under amount.** If your spouse is self-employed in a business or profession, for example as a practicing psychologist who earned $10,500 during the year, you need only show under BLOCK A... "practicing psychologist."

IV. Investment Income

(BLOCKS A and C)

Report items of investment income on the same line of Schedule A as the related property interest or other asset from which income is derived. Note that some property interests or other assets will not have a related item of income. In such a case, check "None (or less than $201)" in BLOCK C under category of amount.

A. Items to Report

Report the identity in BLOCK A and the type and value in BLOCK C of any investment income over $200 from any one source received by or accrued to the benefit of **you, your spouse or dependent child** during the reporting period. For purposes of determining whether you meet the over $200 threshold from any one source, you must aggregate all types of investment income from that same source. For your spouse or dependent child such income is only required to be reported if the asset source meets the reporting threshold in section II above.

Investment income includes, but is not limited to: income derived from dealings in property, interest, rents, royalties, dividends, capital gains; income from annuities, the investment portion of life insurance contracts, or endowment contracts; your distributive share of partnership or joint venture income, gross business income, and income from an interest in an estate or trust. You need not show the actual dollar amount of dividends, rents and royalties, interest, capital gains, or income from qualified trusts, excepted trusts, or excepted investment funds. For these specific types of income, you need only check the category of amount of the item reported of all "other investment income" as described in item

7 below, you will have to report the actual dollar amount of income from each source, and indicate the type in the space marked "Other (specify type)" in BLOCK C.

B. What to Show on the Form

Check all applicable classifications of income and corresponding categories of amounts. If more than one type of income is derived from the same asset, all relevant types (unless an excepted investment fund) and categories of amount. Categories of amount may be distinguished by using the abbreviations D,R,I and CG in the boxes, in lieu of checks, to represent dividends, rents/royalties, interest or capital gains.

1. DIVIDENDS — Show in BLOCK C the amount **you, your spouse or dependent child** accrued or received as dividends from investment sources including common and preferred securities and underlying assets of pension and mutual funds (unless an excepted investment fund). **Identify the source of such income and check the category of amount.** For example, if cash dividends of $950 were received for shares of common stock of IBM, enter in BLOCK A... "IBM common" and in BLOCK C check that dividend income was received and check the appropriate category of amount.

2. RENTS AND ROYALTIES — Show income accrued or received by **you, your spouse or dependent child** as rental or lease payments for occupancy or use of personal or real property in which any one of you has an interest. In addition, show payments accrued or received from such interests as copyrights, royalties, inventions, patents, and mineral leases or other interests. **Identify the source of such income and check the category of amount.** For example, if you received $2,000 as rental income from an apartment building in Miami, Florida, enter in BLOCK A..."apartment building at 5802 Biscayne Blvd., Miami, FL," and in BLOCK C check that rental income was received and check the appropriate category of amount.

3. INTEREST — **Identify the source and the category of amount** of any interest accrued or received by **you, your spouse or dependent child** as income from investment holdings including: bills and notes, loans, personal savings accounts, annuity funds, bonds, and other securities. For example, if you earned $300 in interest during the calendar year on a Savings Certificate with Federal Savings and Loan, enter in BLOCK A..."Federal Savings and Loan (Baltimore, MD)–Savings Certificate," and in BLOCK C check that interest income was received and check the appropriate category of amount.

4. CAPITAL GAINS — Report income from capital gains realized by **you, your spouse or dependent child** from sales or exchanges of property, business interest, partnership interests or securities. **Identify the source and check the category of amount of the gain.** An example of an entry in BLOCK A might be "sale of a one-third interest in 100-acre farm in Hamilton County, Iowa" and in BLOCK C check that capital gains were received and check the appropriate category of amount.

5. INVESTMENT FUND INCOME — **Identify the fund and the category of amount and the type(s) of income** from investment funds such as mutual or pension funds for **you, your spouse or dependent child**. This may include dividends, capital gains and interest for a single fund or income from an excepted investment fund. Income from each individual asset of the fund must also be listed, unless it is an excepted investment fund, in which case income from individual assets is not required to be listed. See Definition of terms above for discussion of excepted investment funds.

6. TRUST INCOME — Report the **category of amount and the type of income** accrued or received from any trust. Whenever you are required to identify the source of trust income, either for **yourself or for a spouse or dependent child,** it is not enough simply to say "John Jones Trust." Generally, the investment holdings of the trust, discussed above under "Property Interests and Assets," and the income derived from each holding must be identified to the same extent as if held directly. However, if the trust is a qualified trust or an excepted trust, in BLOCK A show only the identity of the trust including the date of creation, in BLOCK C check the classification of the trust interest as a "qualified trust" or "excepted trust" and also in BLOCK C show the category of amount of income attributable to you, your spouse or dependent child.

7. OTHER INVESTMENT INCOME — Report any other items of investment income exceeding $200 and not described above, along with the specific type and **actual amount**, such as gross income from business interests, endowment or annuity contract payments, estate income, a distributive share of a partnership or joint business venture income. To identify the sources of other investment income, either for **you, your spouse, or a dependent child**, briefly characterize in BLOCK A the nature of the business or investment interest and, when applicable, the location: for example... "one-third ownership in a retail furniture store at 1010 Grand Ave., Chicago, IL." In BLOCK C under OTHER, specify the applicable type of income, for example... "distributive share" from a partnership or "gross income" from a proprietorship, and under ACTUAL AMOUNT the actual amount of such income which was received during the reporting period. Where the asset is listed because of a value of greater than $1,000 in BLOCK B, but it does not produce more than $200 in income for the reporting period, check "None (or less than $201)" instead of listing the actual amount.

Schedule B

I. Part I—Transactions

A. General Instructions and Items to Report

This part is to be completed by incumbents and termination filers only. Give a description, the date, and the category of amount of any purchase, sale, or exchange of any real property, stocks, bonds, commodity futures, excepted investment fund shares, and other securities by **you, your spouse or dependent child** when the amount involved in the transaction exceeded $1,000. Also, indicate whether sales were made pursuant to a certificate of divestiture previously issued by OGE to permit delayed recognition of capital gain. (For more information on certificates of divestiture, see 5 CFR Part 2634, Subpart J.) This includes reporting any sale or exchange of an asset involving an amount exceeding $1,000 when the sold or exchanged asset did not yield income of more than $200 (and therefore was not reported on Schedule A), or reporting the purchase of an asset involving an amount exceeding $1,000 but at the end of the reporting period having a value of $1,000 or less and earning income of $200 or less during the reporting period (and therefore not appearing on Schedule A). The example on the form shows the proper way to disclose Central Airlines Common Stock the reporting individual purchased for $75,000 on 2/1/91. Note that on Schedule A there is an entry for the stock as well since it was still held at the end of the reporting period.

You need not report a transaction involving (1) your personal residence (unless rented out);(2) a money market account or personal savings account;(3) an asset of your spouse or dependent child if the asset meets the three-part test set forth under the instructions for Schedule A, at II.A.; (4) a holding of a "qualified blind trust," a "qualified diversified trust," or an "excepted trust"; (5) U.S. Treasury bills, notes, and bonds; (6) transactions which occurred prior to your Federal Government employment; or (7) transactions solely by and between the reporting individual, spouse, or dependent child.

You will need to report any transactions made by a non-public business or commercial enterprise, investment pool, or other entity in which you, your spouse or dependent child have a direct proprietary, general partnership or other interest unless (1) the entity is an "excepted investment fund," or (2) the transaction is incidental to the primary trade or business of the entity as indicated by you on Schedule A. (See also sections V.e. and f. of the General Instructions preceding those for Schedule A.)

B. What to Show on the Form

Under identification of assets, identify the property or securities involved in the purchase, sale or exchange, and give the date of the transaction. For example, under IDENTIFICA- TION OF ASSETS... "GMC common stock"; under TYPE OF TRANSACTION... check type; under DATE... enter date transaction occurred; under AMOUNT OF TRANSAC- TION... check the category of value of the sale price, purchase price, or exchange value of the property involved in the transaction. You must also indicate whether an item was sold pursuant to a certificate of divestiture issued by the Office of Government Ethics under 5 CFR Part 2634, Subpart J, to permit delayed recognition of capital gain.

Where multiple transactions have occurred which involve the same asset, you may list the item once, check purchase and/or sale, and indicate... "biweekly," "throughout year," or other appropriate frequency, and the aggregate amount of the sales and purchases. Reporting an exchange generally requires reporting two items since one item is exchanged for another.

II. Part II— Gifts, Reimbursements, and Travel Expenses

A. General Instructions

This Part is to be completed by incumbents and termination filers only. The Act requires you to disclose the receipt of certain gifts, in-kind travel expenses, and travel-related cash reimbursements by **you, your spouse or dependent child** from any one source other than the U.S. Government. This reporting requirement applies to gifts and reimbursements received by your spouse or dependent child to the extent the gift was not given to him or her totally independent of the relationship to you.

B. Items to Report

Report gifts received by **you, your spouse or dependent child** from any one source during the reporting period **aggregating $250 or more,** such as tangible items, or food, lodging, transportation, or entertainment; and travel-related cash reimbursements **aggregating $250 or more** from any one source. A "gift" means any payment, forbearance, advance, ren- dering or deposit of money, or anything of value, unless consideration of equal or greater value is received by the donor. In determining which gifts and reimbursements must be reported or aggregated, **exclude** these items:

1. Anything having a value of $100 or less;

2. Anything received from "relatives" (see Definition of Terms, above);

3. Bequests and other forms of inheritance;

4. Suitable mementos of a function honoring the reporting individual;

5. Food, lodging, transportation, and entertainment or reimbursements provided by a foreign government within a foreign country or by the United States Government, or D.C., state or local governments;

6. Food and beverages not consumed in connection with a gift of overnight lodging;

7. Anything given to a spouse or dependent child totally independent of the relationship to you;

8. Gift items in the nature of communications to your office, such as subscriptions to news- papers and periodicals;

9. Gifts of hospitality (food, lodging, entertainment) on the donor's personal or family premises, as defined in 5 CFR Part 2634;

10. Gifts and reimbursements received during non-Federal employment periods; and

11. Reimbursements you received for political trips which were required to be reported under section 304 of the Federal Election Campaign Act of 1971 (2 U.S.C. § 434).

C. What to Show on the Form

1. GIFTS — Report the identity of the source, a brief description, and the value of gifts aggregating $250 or more from any one source which were received by **you, your spouse or dependent child** and which do not fall within any of the categories of exclusions enumerated above.

a. Food, Lodging, Transportation, Entertainment. Include travel itinerary, dates, and nature of expenses provided. To reach a $250 aggregation, you determine whether any one or combination of the components within this gift category received from one source amounts to $250 or more in value. For example, if you spent a weekend at a hunting lodge owned by AmCoal Corporation, and you received lodging fairly valued at $150, food valued at $115, and entertainment valued at $125, the aggregate value of the gift is $390. A gift of this nature — hospitality at a lodge owned by a corporation rather than an individual — would not qualify as a "personal hospitality" exclusion. To report this gift you would show, under SOURCE... "AmCoal Corp., 1210 North St., Chicago, IL"; under BRIEF DESCRIPTION... "lodging, food, and entertainment as a guest at hunting lodge owned by AmCoal, 1/25–27/91"; and under VALUE... "$390."

b. Other Gifts — If you and your spouse each receive a $175 figurine from the same donor (source), the gifts have a value of more than $250 and must be reported. To report a gift, identify the source, briefly describe the item(s), and show the value. In the case of the figurines, report on the form under SOURCE... "Artifact Co., 153 Utah St., Omaha, NE"; and under BRIEF DESCRIPTION..."two porcelain figurines." Under VALUE..."$350" would be shown.

2. REIMBURSEMENTS — Report the source, a brief description (including a travel itinerary, dates, and the nature of expenses provided), and the value of any cash reimbursements (except those from the United States Government or otherwise excluded) aggregating $250 or more which **you, your spouse or dependent child** received from any one source. For example, if you were reimbursed $400 for travel and lodging expenses in connection with a speech you made for the Denver Realtors Association, you would report this item on the form by showing under SOURCE..."Denver Realtors Assoc., 45 Bridge St., Denver, CO"; under BRIEF DESCRIPTION..."travel expenses for speech made in Denver: United Airlines round trip from Washington, D.C. 1/22–23/91, $275; Denver Airport Marriott, $125"; and under VALUE... "$400" would be shown. If your spouse made this speech and received the reimbursement totally independent of his or her relationship to you, no information for this item need be reported.

Note: If you receive food, transportation, lodging, and entertainment or a reimbursement of official travel expenses from a non-profit tax-exempt institution categorized by the IRS as one falling within the terms of 26 U.S.C. § 501(c)(3), you must report the name of the organization, a brief description of the in-kind services or the reimbursement and the value. If known, you may also wish to note the date you received the required written approval from your agency to accept such items. See 5 U.S.C. § 4111 and 5 CFR Part 410, Subpart G. You do **not** have to report an official reimbursement received **by the agency** since it will not be received by you in your personal capacity (nor by your spouse or dependent child). See 31 U.S.C. § 1353 (or other agency statute) and 41 CFR Parts 301–1 and 304–1.

Schedule C

I. Part I—Liabilities

A. General Instructions

The Act requires you to disclose certain of your financial liabilities. The examples on the form show how to report a mortgage on real estate the reporting individual held for the production of income and a promissory note. Note that you will need to disclose the date, interest rate and term (if applicable) of each liability. Also note you must disclose the highest amount owed on any liability held during the reporting period, not just at the end of the period. If the liability was completely paid during the period, you may also note that on the form if you wish.

B. Items to Report

Identify and give the category of amount of the liabilities which **you, your spouse or dependent child** owed to any creditor which exceeded $10,000 at any time during the reporting period, **except:**

1. a personal liability owed to a spouse or dependent child, or to a parent, brother, sister, or child of you, your spouse or dependent child;

2. a mortgage or home equity loan secured by real property which is the personal residence (or a second residence not used for producing income) of you or your spouse;

3. a loan secured by a personal motor vehicle, household furniture, or appliances, where the loan does not exceed the purchase price of the item;

4. a revolving charge account where the outstanding liability did not exceed $10,000 as of the close of the reporting period; and

5. any liability of your spouse or dependent child which represents the sole financial interest or responsibility of the spouse or child, and about which you have no knowledge, and which is not derived from your income, assets, or activities, and concerning which you neither derive nor expect to derive any financial or economic benefit.

You are required to report any liability of any non-public company, investment pool, or other entity, in which you, your spouse or dependent child have an interest, unless (1) the liability is incidental to the primary trade or business of the entity as indicated by you on Schedule A, or (2) the entity is an excepted investment fund. (See also sections V.e. and f. of the General Instructions preceding those for Schedule A.)

C. What to Show on the Form

Under CREDITORS (NAME AND ADDRESS), show the name and address of the actual creditor unless the reporting individual is only able to identify a fiduciary and certifies in the report that he has made a good faith effort to determine who the actual creditor is and was unable to do so, or upon his certification that such determination is otherwise impracticable. Under TYPE OF LIABILITY, briefly indicate the nature of the liability. Under DATE, enter date loan incurred; under INTEREST RATE, note the set rate or, if a variable one, the formula used to vary the rate, i.e. Prime +2%; and under TERM, show the duration of the loan. Check the category of value for the highest amount owed during the reporting period.

II. Part II — Agreements or Arrangements

A. General Instructions and Items to Report

Provide information regarding any agreements or arrangements you have concerning (1) future employment; (2) a leave of absence during your period of Government service; (3) continuation of payments by a former employer other than the United States Government; and (4) continuing participation in an employee welfare or benefit plan maintained by a former employer other than United States Government retirement benefits. This includes any agreements or arrangements with a future employer entered into by a termination filer. The example on the form shows the severance agreement under which the reporting individual expects to receive a lump sum payment from the law firm he has left in order to enter the Government.

For purposes of public disclosure, you must disclose any negotiations for future employment from the point you and a potential non-Federal employer have agreed to your future employment by that employer whether or not you have settled all of the terms, such as salary, title, benefits, and date employment is to begin. Your agency may require internal disclosure of negotiations much earlier and you should seek guidance before conducting any negotiations with persons with whom you do business. A criminal statute, 18 U.S.C. § 208, applies to official actions you may take while negotiating future employment.

B. What to Show on the Form

Under STATUS AND TERMS, describe the agreement or arrangement with appropriate specificity. Under PARTIES, show the name of the organization, or entity, and (if applicable) the name and title of the official, corporate officer, or principal person responsible for carrying out the terms of the agreement or arrangement. Under DATE, show the date of any such arrangement. **No report is required regarding any agreement or arrangement entered into by a spouse or dependent child.**

Schedule D

I. Part I—Outside Positions

A. Items to Report

Report all outside positions held at any time during the reporting period, as well as those positions you currently hold as an officer, director, trustee, general partner, proprietor, representative, employee or consultant of (1) any corporation, company, firm, partnership, trust, or other business enterprise; (2) any non-profit organization; (3) any labor organization; (4) any educational institution; or (5) any organization other than the United States Government. **Exclude** positions held in any religious, social, fraternal, or political entity, and any positions solely of an honorary nature. Be sure to report on Schedule A any income over $200 that you received from acting in any of these positions. **No report is required regarding any positions held by your spouse or dependent child.**

B. What to Show on the Form

Give the name, address and brief description (type) of the organization, the title or other brief functional description of the position, and the dates you held the position. If you currently hold the position, in the entry block under TO, note "Present."

II. Part II—Compensation in Excess of $5,000 Paid by One Source

A. General Instructions

This Part is to be completed by nominees and new entrants only. You must disclose your sources of compensation in excess of $5,000 and the nature of the duties you provided. This includes not only the source of your salary or other fees, but the disclosure of clients for whom you personally provided $5,000 or more in services even though the clients' payments were made to your employer, firm or other business affiliation. The examples on the form show the proper way to disclose the business affiliation which paid the reporting individual's compensation, in this case a law firm, and a client of the firm for which the reporting individual personally provided over $5,000 worth of services. This Part does not require you to disclose the value of the compensation for these services; it does require a brief description of the services you provided. When a source has paid you directly, you should have a corresponding entry on Schedule A if the payment was within the reporting period for Schedule A. A client who paid your business affiliation more than $5,000 for your services will appear only in this Part.

B. Items to Report

Report the nature of the duties performed or services rendered for any person (other than the United States Government) from which compensation in excess of $5,000 in either of the two preceding calendar years or the present calendar year was received by you or an entity which billed for your services (business affiliation). **Exclude:** (1) information to the extent that it is considered confidential as a result of a privileged relationship established by law, or (2) information about persons for whom "services were provided by a business affiliation of which you were a member, partner or employee unless you were directly involved in the provision of the services. The name of a client of a law firm is not generally considered confidential. **No report is required regarding compensation paid to your spouse or a dependent child.**

C. What to Show on the Form

Under SOURCE, give the name and address of the person to whom services were provided, for example, "Newark Real Estate Co. (Newark, NJ)"; and under BRIEF DESCRIPTION, the title or other brief functional description of the services rendered, for example "tax matters researched for above firm while an associate with Quinn and Ouspensky."

Privacy Act Statement

Title I of the Ethics in Government Act of 1978, as amended (the "Act"), 5 U.S.C. app. § 101 et seq., and 5 C.F.R. Part 2634 of the Office of Government Ethics regulations require the reporting of this information. The primary use of the information on this report is for review by Government officials to determine compliance with applicable Federal laws and regulations. This report may also be disclosed upon request to any requesting person pursuant to section 105 of the Act or as otherwise authorized by law. You may inspect applications for public access of your own form upon request. Additional disclosures of the information on this report may be made: (1) to a Federal, State, or local law enforcement agency if the disclosing agency becomes aware of a violation or potential violation of law or regulation; (2) to a court or party in a court or Federal administrative proceeding if the Government is a party or in order to comply with a judge-issued subpoena; (3) to a source when necessary to obtain information relevant to a conflict of interest investigation or decision; (4) to the National Archives and Records Administration or the General Services Administration in records management inspections; (5) to the Office of Management and Budget during legislative coordination on private relief legislation; and (6) in response to a request for discovery or for the appearance of a witness in a judicial or administrative proceeding, if the information is relevant to the subject matter. See also the OGE/GOVT-1 executive branch-wide Privacy Act system of records. Knowing and willful falsification of information, or failure to file or report information required to be reported by section 102 of the Act, may subject you to a civil penalty of not more than $10,000 and to disciplinary action by your employing agency or other appropriate authority under section 104 of the Act.

Knowing and willful falsification of information required to be filed by section 102 of the Act may also subject you to criminal prosecution.

Public Burden Information

This collection of information is estimated to take an average of three hours per response, including time for reviewing the instructions, gathering the data needed, and completing the form. Send comments regarding the burden estimate or any other aspect of this collection of information, including suggestions for reducing this burden, to the Associate Director for Administration, U.S. Office of Government Ethics, Suite 500, 1201 New York Avenue, NW., Washington, DC 20005–3917; and to the Office of Management and Budget, Paperwork Reduction Project (3209-0001), Washington, DC 20503. **Do not file** financial disclosure reports at these addresses; submit them as indicated in "Where to File" on page 3.

Fee for Late Filing

Any individual who is required to file this report and does so more than 30 days after the date the report is required to be filed, or, if an extension is granted, more than 30 days after the last day of the filing extension period shall be subject to a $200 late filing fee. A report is considered to be filed when it is received by the agency. Such fee will be collected by the filer's agency, for deposit with the U.S. Treasury.

INDEX

Abusiveness: of appointment process, 6–7, 64, 77–78, 101; of confirmation process, 21–22, 105, 106, 127; reducing, 21–23, 73–74
Accountability: presidential, 18
Acheson, Dean, 104
Achtenberg, Roberta, 64, 148
AFL-CIO, 111
Aleinkoff, Alex, 145
Alliance for Justice, 154
American Bar Association, 104, 111, 133
Appointment process, 37, 49, 90–91, 159–60; delays in, 13; politicalization of, 100–102, 130, 137, 152–54; problems with, 3, 4–8, 67, 99–100, 159; procedures in, 47, 67; purpose of, 4, 158–59; recommendations for, 8–17, 21–23, 74–78; standards in, 75, 144. *See also* Confirmation process; Clearance process; Presidential appointees; Recuitment of nominees
Aron, Nan, 133, 154

Babbitt, Bruce, 89, 140, 149
Background checks of nominees, 3, 55–58, 75–76, 141; recommendations for, 11, 14–16, 76
Baird, Zoë, 64, 70–71, 92, 141–44

Baker, Howard, 125
Battle for Justice (Bronner), 93
Bauer, Gary, 134
Bidden, Joseph, 125, 134–35, 136, 141, 142
Black, Hugo, 103–104
Blackburn, Ben, 119
Blackmun, Harry, 95, 114, 149
Bode, Ken, 102, 156, 158
Bolick, Clint, 144, 145, 152, 153, 159–60
Bork, Robert, 71, 93, 95, 97, 102, 125–27, 137, 146–47, 148
Brandeis, Louis, 77
Brennan, William J., 105, 132
Breyer, Stephen, 89, 91–92, 93, 156, 158, 167 n8
Broder, David, 143–44, 155
Bronner, Ethan, 93, 126–27
Brown, Hank, 147
Brown, Sam, 147, 153
Burger, Warren, 114, 124
Burt, Richard, 123
Bush, George, 75, 77, 119, 129, 132, 143–44, 154
Bush administration, 4–5, 6, 17; appointees, 97, 129–37, 146–47, 151
Butz, Earl, 119

Cabinet: appointees, 77–79, 99, 119, 121–22, 123–24, 129–32, 140–44, 148, 151–52

ABOUT THE AUTHORS

G. CALVIN MACKENZIE holds a Ph.D. in government from Harvard University and is Distinguished Presidential Professor of American Government at Colby College. He is author or editor of more than a dozen books, including *The Politics of Presidential Appointments, The In-and-Outers,* and *The Irony of Reform: Roots of American Political Disenchantment.* He has been a congressional staff member, a consultant to several federal agencies, and a soldier with the First Cavalry Division in Vietnam. He currently serves as chair of the Maine Commission on Governmental Ethics and Election Practices.

ROBERT SHOGAN has been national political correspondent for the *Los Angeles Times* since 1973. He is the author of several books on politics and government, including *Hard Bargain, The Riddle of Power,* and *Promises to Keep.*